Matheus Zulian dos Santos

WILDLIFE TRADE AND BIODIVERSITY CONSERVATION

AF209888

Matheus Zulian dos Santos

WILDLIFE TRADE AND BIODIVERSITY CONSERVATION

IMPACTS, REGULATION AND ENFORCEMENT

ScienciaScripts

Imprint
Any brand names and product names mentioned in this book are subject to trademark, brand or patent protection and are trademarks or registered trademarks of their respective holders. The use of brand names, product names, common names, trade names, product descriptions etc. even without a particular marking in this work is in no way to be construed to mean that such names may be regarded as unrestricted in respect of trademark and brand protection legislation and could thus be used by anyone.

Cover image: www.ingimage.com

This book is a translation from the original published under ISBN 978-620-2-56114-3.

Publisher:
Sciencia Scripts
is a trademark of
Dodo Books Indian Ocean Ltd. and OmniScriptum S.R.L publishing group

120 High Road, East Finchley, London, N2 9ED, United Kingdom
Str. Armeneasca 28/1, office 1, Chisinau MD-2012, Republic of Moldova, Europe
Managing Directors: Ieva Konstantinova, Victoria Ursu
info@omniscriptum.com

Printed at: see last page
ISBN: 978-620-2-70390-1

MACKENZIE PRESBYTERIAN UNIVERSITY

CENTER FOR SCIENCE AND TECHNOLOGY - LAW COURSE

MATHEUS ZULIAN DOS SANTOS

WILDLIFE TRADE AND BIODIVERSITY CONSERVATION: IMPACTS,
REGULATION AND ENFORCEMENT

CAMPINS

2019

MATHEUS ZULIAN DOS SANTOS

WILDLIFE TRADE AND BIODIVERSITY CONSERVATION: IMPACTS,
REGULATION AND ENFORCEMENT

Course Conclusion Work presented to the
Graduate Course in Law, from
Universidade Presbiteriana Mackenzie a
mandatory requirement for obtaining a
Bachelor's degree.

Advisor: Professor Dr. Márcia Brandão Lion Sheep

CAMPINS
2019

MATHEUS ZULIAN DOS SANTOS

WILDLIFE TRAFFICKING AND BIODIVERSITY CONSERVATION: IMPACTS, REGULATION AND ENFORCEMENT.

Course Conclusion Work presented to the Graduate Course in Law, from Universidade Presbiteriana Mackenzie a mandatory requirement for obtaining a Bachelor's degree.

Approved on:

EXAMINATION COMMISSION

_____

Professor Dr. Marcia Brandão Lion Sheep

_____

INVITED 1

_____

INVITED 2

_____

COURSE COORDINATOR

To the teacher Dr. Márcia, for her patience in orientation, conviviality, understanding, que made possible a the conclusion of this work.

ACKNOWLEDGEMENTS

I thank the people in my life that I love and have given me support and love. to my mother, an example to be followed. To my girlfriend, for all the support in the hardest times, for all the time and affection dedicated, comfort and encouragement in the hard times, of discouragement e tiredness. And a special hug to my grandparents, who made me love nature and the countryside.

"The greatness of a nation can be judged by the way its animals are treated." (Mahatma Gandhi)

SUMMARY

This study aims to analyse the impact of wildlife trafficking on biodiversity and the legal and institutional forecasts for combating it. Brazil, a megabiodiverse country, finds it difficult to combat the existing crimes of trafficking, putting all fauna at risk. Therefore, the present study analyses this issue as follows: the first chapter deals with the environment and its conceptions; the second chapter addresses international protection and Brazilian legislation on the subject; and, finally, armed with all the previous construction, the last chapter mentions the issue of wildlife trafficking, the conceptual part, the impacts, the combat and possible methods to reduce the problem.

Keywords: Criminal Law. Fauna. Animal trafficking.

ABSTRACT

This study aims to analyze the impact of wildlife trafficking on biodiversity and the legal and institutional predictions for its combat. Brazil, a megabiodiversity country, finds it difficult to combat existing trafficking crimes, endangering all fauna. Thus, the present study analyzes this issue, as follows: The first chapter deals with the environment and its conceptions, the second deals with international protection and the Brazilian legislation related to the theme. And finally, with all the previous construction, the last chapter comes to mention the theme of wildlife trafficking, the conceptual part, the impacts, the combat and possible methods to reduce the problem.

Keywords: Criminal law. Fauna. Animal trafficking.

SUMMARY

1. INTRODUCTION

This study aims to analyse the difficulties of controlling and punishing animal trafficking, which has terrible effects on the conservation and balance of the planet's biodiversity. The work was focused on specific legislation on the subject, and one of the most relevant is the Environmental Crimes Law, which brought with it a completeness with regard to the normatization of illegal activities and their respective penalties.

Brazil, as we know, has an immense biodiversity and is extremely rich in fauna species. Thus, animal trafficking threatens all this natural wealth, and the existing penalties are very light and effective, not achieving the desired effect.

Environmental Law is a branch of law whose importance stands out in the preservation and conservation of the biological balance, relying on the existence, including criminal rules, in order to inhibit and combat threats to the natural environment.

Wildlife trafficking is among the world's largest illegal trades, second only to arms and drug trafficking. The animals are removed from the forests and forests and the actions involved in this activity destroy the Brazilian fauna.   The trafficking of animals is not adequately foreseen in the specific penal legislation (Environmental Crimes Law), which makes the punishment of this activity difficult.

The Brazilian territorial dimension and the deficiencies in the inspection systems - besides the low awareness of the social conscience regarding the importance of biodiversity - are additional difficulties regarding the issue, which demonstrates the importance of the study.

The first chapter will deal with the environment and biodiversity; the second will address international protection and Brazilian legislation on the subject.

Next, the topic of wildlife trafficking, the impacts of this activity, the fight and possible methods to deal with it as a problem will be addressed.

Fauna is important for the balance of the ecosystem and the conservation of biodiversity, and, to this end, all means must be used to curb, control and exterminate animal trafficking, which ranges from better monitoring to international support, as will be seen at the end of this context.

2. ENVIRONMENT AND BIODIVERSITY

The concept of the environment is much broader than one can imagine, and goes far beyond possible reflections on the natural and wild environment.

In the 1988 Constitution, Article 225 is dedicated to the environment and in its "caput" it states that

> Everyone has the right to an ecologically balanced environment, a good for the common use of the people and essential to a healthy quality of life, imposing on the Public Power and the collectivity the duty to defend it and preserve it for present and future generations.[1]

In addition, the FC and other national laws distinguish between each type of environment as follows: cultural, artificial, natural and work environment. In this way, the cultural environment integrates the artistic, landscape, archaeological, historical and tourist heritage - corresponding to art. 225, § 1° and § 2°.

The artificial environment (art. 5, XXIII, art. 21, XX CF) can be understood as that which encompasses all human achievements, that is, all spaces built by man, because it is the fruit of the direct actions of man, which alter, transform and modify the natural environmental characteristics, causing the loss of the untouched originality of the natural environment[2]. The cultural environment presents itself as a reflection of human capacity, represents the result of immaterial and material culture generated by societies through customs, human interactions, thus generating a cultural asset that is protected by the Federal Constitution due to its importance for present and future generations, because it carries the identity of its people[3].

The natural environment (art. 225, § 1, I and VII CF) can be identified in the National Environmental Policy Law - Law n° 6.938/1981 - in its art. 3°, item I, thus described: "The set of conditions, laws, influences and interactions of physical, chemical and biological order, which allows, shelters and regulates life in all its forms"[4].

---

[1]BRAZIL. *1988 Constitution of the Federative Republic of Brazil*. Brasília/DF, 1988. Available at: < http://www.planalto.gov.br/ccivil_03/constituicao/constituicao.htm>. Access on: 18 Nov. 2019.
[2]BECHARA, Erika. *The protection of fauna from the constitutional point of view*. São Paulo: Juarez de Oliveira, 2003, p. 11.
[3]*Ibid*, p. 09-10.
[4]BRAZIL. *Law No. 6938, of August 31, 1981*. Provides on the National Environmental Policy, its purposes and mechanisms of formulation and application, and makes other provisions. Brasília/DF, 1981, art. 3. Available at: <http://www.planalto.gov.br/ccivil_03/Leis/L6938.htm>. Access on: 06 mar. 2019.

The referred article also brings in its clauses a series of natural resources essential to the maintenance of its quality.

Furthermore, the work environment, which is cited by the Constitution in its art. 200, item VIII, must be understood as the place where one works, that is, performs a task, a trade, of which the standards to be adopted to achieve a healthy balance in human work conditions must be the best possible, maintaining the safety and health of the worker in dignified conditions that respect the human condition and the value of life5.

The concept, however, about the whole that composes the natural environment, among the others, is what leads to the original aspect of the environment, untouched, wild, immaculate by man, following only the laws of nature, the natural order of life in all its aspects, gathering all species and forms of life in the world.

Bringing this concept to the Brazilian border limitations on the natural environment, the legislator formulated a definition that sought, in addition to conceptualization, to achieve more concrete definitions, pointing in a direction that provides for the protection of the natural environment.

The concept of environment is therefore quite broad, far beyond the natural environment, the object of this study, which will be dedicated to analyze the concept of biodiversity and the importance of its protection, given the threat posed by animal trafficking.

2.1. FAUNA, FLORA AND BIODIVERSITY

The concept of Fauna can be found in legal text and positived by Law No. 5,197 of 1967, which provides for the protection of fauna. The concept designates a group of animals belonging to natural life, free, that inhabit a certain region6.

> Art. 1. Animals of any species, at any stage of their development and that live naturally outside of captivity, constituting wild fauna, as well as their nests, shelters and natural breeding grounds are property of the

---

5BECHARA, Erika. *The protection of fauna from the constitutional point of view*. São Paulo: Juarez de Oliveira, 2003, p. 13-14.
6BRAZIL. Ministry of Environment. *Glossary*. Available at: <http://www.mma.gov.br/component/k2/item/430-gloss>. Access on: 10 jun. 2019.

State, and their use, persecution, destruction, hunting or harvesting is prohibited.[7]

As a native or autochthonous species, any species that appears in a region as a result of a natural phenomenon, without the intervention of the human being, can be considered. An introduced or exotic species[8] is a non-native species that was introduced in an ecosystem[9], being this understood as the whole of the living beings and the place they inhabit in perfect balance; but when the exotic species is affected by factors different from its environment, either by human action accidentally or deliberately, it generates negative effects. Finally, the invasive species are those that establish a new region, either as a result of a natural phenomenon or as a result of human action, but which usually end up, in both cases, producing negative changes in the composition of the ambientenatural[10].

Flora is conceptualized as a group of organisms of the plant kingdom present in a certain place, a region of its own ecosystem, carrying several characteristics. In Brazil, the diversity of flora is incredibly gigantic, since here the most varied ecosystems are present, such as the Amazon Forest, Atlantic Forest, Cerrado, among others; each one carrying peculiarities characterized by the adaptation of the climate where it is inserted[11].

In this respect, fauna and flora are closely linked and interdependent. It is through the plant kingdom, in its most varied forms, that a chain of species from the animal kingdom, belonging to the Fauna, remains alive, feeding itself, seeking refuge, reproducing itself and even keeping the Flora alive when, for example, when feeding itself, the Fauna takes the seeds of the Flora to other places through excretion or simply dropping them somewhere.

Nature is governed by its own guidelines, its cyclical natural laws, that is, circular, since it reuses its own resources through recycling: the famous natural

[7]Id. Law No. 5,197 of January 3, 1967. Provides on the protection of fauna and makes other provisions. Brasília, 1967. Available at: <http://www.planalto.gov.br/c civil_03/leis/L5197.htm>. Access on: 05 mar. 2019.
[8]BRAZIL. Ministry of the Environment, loc. cit.
[9]Ibid.
[10]Ibid.
[11]Id. Flora is recognized as one of the most important in the world. Brazil Legacy, Environment, Plant Species, 11 Apr. 2012. Available at: <http://www.brasil.gov.br/noticias/meioambiente/2012/04/flora-brasileira>. Accessed on: 04 Jun. 2019.

decomposition, based on a law not written to human eyes, but only possible to be observed and felt. The imbalance resulting from human intelligence employed in an ill-considered manner in the environment corrupts the natural balance and generates degradation.

The natural wealth is so expressive that it exceeds by 90% the quantity of organisms that humanity is unaware of. Among 1.4 million catalogued and studied, 750,000 would be insects, 41,000 vertebrates and 250,000 plants. Particularly the insects, taken by sampling from the Amazon rainforest, showed that in a global estimate in tropical forests there would be thirty million species of insects[12].

The most studied groups in fauna are vertebrates, and in flora, plants with flowers, in temperate regions[13].

The cataloguing carried out by biologists follows descriptive patterns and aims, mainly, to study the diversity of species and their function in the ecosystem.

Brazil has the most diverse biomes on the planet, including the Cerrado, the Amazon Rainforest, which are included in our Magna Carta (Article 225, § 4), and others, making Brazil the country with the greatest biodiversity in the world, representing 20% of all existing species. There are also species that, due to the particularities existing in the Brazilian biomes, have developed solely on homeland soil, making biodiversity very rare and varied[14].

In 2018, the Brazilian government, with the participation of several technical experts, launched through the Ministry of the Environment the Red Book of Brazilian Fauna - Animals Threatened with Extinction, pointing out the degree of risk of extinction of the listed species and listing the main causes of harmful impacts to nature[15].

Brazil is a country of **continental proportions**: its **8.5 million square kilometers** occupy almost **half of South America and encompass**

[12]BARBIERI, Edison. *Biodiversity*: the variety of life on planet Earth: Current knowledge about biodiversity. South Coast Research and Development Unit (Cananéia), of the Advanced Center for Technology Research of Marine Fisheries Agribusiness, Instituto de Pesca, Apta (Paulista Agency for Agribusiness Technology), Secretariat of Agriculture and Supply of the State of São Paulo, São Paulo, p. 1-16, 2010. Available at: <https://www.pesca.sp.gov.br/biodiversidade.pdf>. Accessed on: 04 Jun. 2019.
[13]*Ibid.*
[14]BRAZIL. Ministry of Environment. *Brazilian Biodiversity*. Available at: <http://www.mma.gov.br/biodiversidade/biodiversidade-brasileira>. Access on: 11 jun. 2019.
[15]*Id*. Red Book of the Brazilian Fauna Threatened with Extinction. Brasília: ICMBIO, 2018. Available at: <http://www.icmbio.gov.br/portal/images/stories/comunicacao/publicacoes/publicacoes-diversas/livro_vermelho_2018_vol1.pdf>. Accessed on: 03 jun. 2019.

several climate zones - such as the humid tropic in the North, the semi-arid in the Northeast and temperate areas in the South. Of course, these climatic differences lead to great **ecological variations**, forming **distinct biogeographical zones or biomes:** the Amazon Rainforest, the largest humid tropical forest in the world; the Pantanal, the largest floodplain; the savannah and woodland Cerrado; the Caatinga of semiarid forests; the fields of the Pampas; and the rainforest of the Atlantic Forest. In addition, Brazil has a marine coast of 3.5 million km², which includes ecosystems such as coral reefs, dunes, mangroves, lagoons, estuaries and swamps.

The variety of biomes reflects the enormous wealth of Brazilian flora and fauna: **Brazil is home to the planet's greatest biodiversity.** This abundant variety of life - which translates into more than **20% of the total number of species on Earth** - elevates Brazil to the rank of the leading nation among the 17 mega diverse (or most biodiverse) countries.

Occupying **the 1st position in total number of species, with approximately 3 thousand species of terrestrial vertebrates and 3 thousand of freshwater fish.** It is also the **richest** country in **mammal diversity in the world with 483 continental and 41 marine species, totaling 524 species. In birds, it occupies the 3rd position with about 1677 species, being 1524 residents and 153 visitors. In reptiles, it ranks 4th with about 468 species and 1st in number of amphibians with about 517 species.**

These numbers have only been increasing because new Brazilian species continue to be described. Since 1990, 10 new primate species have been discovered in Brazil. The most recent ones, Callithrixmanicorensis and Callithrixacariensis, were found in 1996 in Amazonian communities where they were bred as pets, although they are still unknown to science. New species of birds were also discovered, one in 1995 in the coast of the state of Paraná, obicudinho-do-brejo, Stymphalornisacutirostris, and in 1998, the macuquinho-da-várzea, Scytalopusiraiensis [16] (Griffon vulture)

Biodiversity, by definition, means diversity of life, or biological diversity would be the vast number of living forms on our planet Earth[17].

In biodiversity are present all the living forms of the planet, with their genetic variety and the respective ecological functions they perform in the environment.

The concept of species means a set of individuals that can cross each other, perpetuating themselves. An ecosystem, on the other hand, specifies the variety of populations of species that cohabit in a certain region, taking advantage of local

---

[16]RENCTAS. *1st National Report on Wildlife Trafficking.* Available at: <http://renctas.org.br/wpcontent/uploads/2014/02/REL_RENCTAS_pt_final.pdf>. Access on: 06 mar. 2019.

[17]BRAZIL. Ministry of Environment. *Glossary.* Available at: <http://www.mma.gov.br/component/k2/item/430-gloss>. Access on: 10 jun. 2019.

resources. To accurately determine these factors requires investment by the country in appropriate research methods in order to faithfully achieve knowledge of its biodiversity, responding to international reports of studies, cataloguing and preservation of species[18].

The concept of biodiversity is very recent, was thought by Walter G. Rosen in 1985, while organizing a forum on biological diversity, which was held in Washington, capital of the United States, from September 21 to 24, 1986, under the name of National Forum on Biodiversity, concerned with its conservation[19].

Later, in 1992, the Convention on Biological Diversity - which will be discussed below - refers to biodiversity (biological diversity) in its Article 2 as:

> [...] the variability of living organisms from all sources, including, among others, terrestrial, marine and other aquatic ecosystems and the ecological complexes of which they are part; including diversity within species, between species and of ecosystems.[20]

Therefore, taking into consideration the interdependence of species and their relationship with Humanity, and considering their importance in terms of the economic activities developed by society, its value should be considered as follows.

2.2. THE ECONOMIC VALUE OF BIODIVERSITY

---

[18]BIODIVERSITY. Brazil: Uesc. Available at: <http://nead.uesc.br/arquivos/Biologia/modulo_8bl oco_1/uni_biodiversity_ecology/support_material/M8EBU1_biodiversity.pdf>. Access on: 02 jun. 2019.

[19]FRANCO, José Luiz de Andrade. The concept of biodiversity and the history of conservation biology: from wilderness preservation to biodiversity conservation. *History*, São Paulo, v. 32, 2013, p. 21-48. Available at: <http://www.scielo.br/pdf/his/v32n2/a03v32n2.pdf>. Access on: 04 jun. 2019.

[20]BRAZIL. *Decree No. 2519 of March 16, 1998.* The Convention on Biological Diversity. Brasília/DF, 1998. Available at: <http://www.planalto.gov.br/ccivil_03/decreto/D2519.htm>. Access on: 06 mar. 2019.

[21]As early as 1987, the Report of the United Nations World Commission on the Environment, called "Our Common Future",[22]stated that

> Wild species contribute to medicine. Half of all avian recipes originate from wild organisms. The commercial value of these medicines and drugs in the U.S. today reaches about $14 billion annually. In global terms, including non-prescription substances and pharmaceuticals, the estimated commercial value exceeds $40 billion per year.[23]

The Report presents the concept of Sustainable Development as follows: "Sustainable development is that which meets the needs of the present without compromising the ability of future generations to meet their own needs[24]. For it is observed that when a population is stabilized at a level compatible with the productive capacity of the ecosystem, there is no excessive exploitation of the natural environment, giving time for it to regenerate and reach a balance again.

According to the TEEB Report, in order to evaluate an environmental resource one must consider:

> The value of direct use that implies the immediate consumption of the good;
>
> The value of indirect use that are services of tourism, decarbon sequestration, research, etc.;
>
> The option value: direct and indirect use in the future; and
>
> The value of existence linked to cultural, ethical, moral, spiritual comfort issues, etc.
>
> The total economic value would be the sum of all these values.[25]

---

[21]The United Nations, also known by its acronym UN, is an international organisation formed by countries that have voluntarily come together to work for peace and world development. UN (UNITED NATIONS ORGANIZATION - UN. Meet the UN. Available at: <https://nacoesunidas.org/conheca/>. Accessed on: 25 Oct. 2019).
[22]WORLD COMMISSION ON ENVIRONMENT AND DEVELOPMENT - CMMAD. *Our Common Future*. 2. ed. Rio de Janeiro: Fundação Getúlio Vargas, 1991, p. 171.
[23]*Ibid.*
[24]ORGANIZATION OF THE UNITED NATIONS - UN. *Brundtland Report* - Our Common Future. 2. ed. Rio de Janeiro: Fundação Getúlio Vargas, 1991. p. 46. Available at: <https://edisciplinas.usp.br/pluginfile.php/4245128/mod_resource/content/3/Nosso%20Futuro%20Comum.pdf>. Access on: 10 nov. 2019.
[25]Led by the United Nations Environment Programme (UNEP), the TEEB initiative was launched in 2007 at a meeting of the G8+5, a group that brings together the leaders of the G8 countries (Canada, France, Germany, Italy, Japan, Russia, the United Kingdom and the United States) and the G5 countries (South Africa, Brazil, China, India and Mexico).

In this sense, the report highlights that biodiversity provides a number of services that can be classified as follows: Relationship between biodiversity; Provisioning Services - e.g. wild food, plantations, water and plant-derived remedies; Regulation Services - e.g. the filtration of pollutants by wetlands, climate regulation by carbon storage and water cycle, pollination and disaster protection; Cultural Services - e.g. recreation, spiritual and aesthetic values, education; Support Services - e.g. soil formation, photosynthesis and nutrient cycling26,

> The concepts of ecosystem services and natural capital can help us recognize the many benefits provided by nature. From an economic perspective, ecosystem services flows can be seen as the "dividend" society receives from natural capital. Maintaining stocks of natural capital enables the sustainable provision of future flows of ecosystem services, and thus contributes to ensuring permanent human well-being.27

According to the Business Sector Report: Avoiding Greenhouse Gas emissions through forest conservation could mean about US$ 3.7 trillion; the contribution of pollinating insects to results in agriculture could be estimated at approximately US$ 190 billion/year and 25-50% of the US$ 640 billion in the pharmaceutical market comes from genetic resources.

Other projections in the same report for 2050 point to a market of US$ 900 billion for certified agricultural products; US$ 50 billion for certified forest products and US$ 20 billion for water-related services; US$ 500 billion from bioprospecting (research with genetic resources), among others.

Considered a major step in the conservation of the planet, the TEBB (The Economics of Ecosystems and Biodiversity) aims to assess the economic benefit of biological diversity, the costs of loss of this biodiversity and the relationship between the lack of investment in preventive actions and the costs of effective conservation of biodiversity (THE ECONOMICS OF ECOSYSTEMS AND BIODIVERSITY - TEEB). *Business Sector Report* - Executive Summary   01-07-2010.   Available   at: <http://www.mma.gov.br/publicacoes/biodiversidade/category/143-economia-dos-ecossistemas-e-da-biodiversidade.html?download=968:teeb-sumario-executivo>. Accessed on: 25 Oct. 2019).
26THE ECONOMICS OF ECOSYSTEMS AND BIODIVERSITY - TEEB. *Report for the Business   Sector   -   Executive   Summary   01-07-2010.   Available   at:* <http://www.mma.gov.br/publicacoes/biodiversidade/category/143-economia-dos-ecossistemas-e-da-biodiversidade.html?download=968:teeb-sumario-executivo>. Accessed on: 25 Oct. 2019
27*Ibid.*

However, it is necessary to register that only a philosophical vision with a broader perception of life can recognize that the value of the environment is not only monetary, but the so-called principles or values of human beings.

> Man needs the goods that exist in the world in order to live. In view of this, the right arises, so that there may be ordering of these goods, at the risk of making impossible the relations between people who would be involved in the greatest anarchy, Valor, from this perspective, is what has meaning.
>
> It has "value" because it is appreciated, understood, admitted, loved and therefore needs to be recognized and preserved, in a word, protected. We are interested in a good and therefore it becomes the object of the right. The right exists for the protection of values.[28]

By assigning the meanings to the world around us, a value is also assigned. The environment is among those values that give rise to conflict, often putting economics and ethics in opposition:

> Generally, it is not recognized that values are not peripheral to science and technology, but constitute their own basis and driving force. During the scientific revolution in the 17th century, values were separated from facts, and since that time we tend to believe that scientific facts are independent of what we do, and are therefore independent of our values. In reality, scientific facts emerge from a whole constellation of human perceptions, values and actions - in a word, they emerge from a paradigm - from which they cannot be separated. While much of the detailed research may not depend explicitly on the scientist's value system, the broader paradigm within which this research is conducted will never be value-free. Therefore, scientists are responsible for their research not only intellectually but also morally. Within the context of deep ecology, the view that these values are inherent in all living nature is founded on deep experience, ecological or spiritual, that nature and the self are one.[29]

Analyzing the above quotation it is possible to identify the difficulty to stipulate a cash valuation to natural life, or even to compare these natural reserves to a raw material stock. However, this reasoning is common in society because it is based on

---

[28]ANDRADE FILHO, Álvaro Ricardo Azevedo; CALÇADO, Gustavo Silva. *Law as value*. São Paulo:Aprombh. Available at: <http://www.aprombh.com.br/artigos/1218-direito-enquanto-valor>. Accessed on: 03 jun. 2019.
[29]CAPRA, Fritjof. *The web of life*: a new scientific understanding of living systems. São Paulo: Cultrix. cap.1, p. 20. Available at: <http://www.communita.com.br/assets/teiadavi dafritjofcapra.pdf>. Access on: 08 Jun. 2019.

the exchange of goods and services valued in monetary units and available to an individual called consumer.

It is observed that biodiversity is offered as a product not differentiated from another, accepted as a commodity by human rationalization. In this context, the concept of development of nations has for a long time - and still does so intensely - accepted the indiscriminate consumption of natural resources in exchange for raising the level of a doubtful well-being of their societies.

Even with the emergence of systemic thinking in the 20th century, which considers the properties of an organism as an indivisible whole, many nations hope that it will be possible to equate economic growth to the maximum with the preservation of biodiversity:

> The great impact that came with 20th century science was the perception that systems cannot be understood by analysis. The properties of the parts are not intrinsic properties, but can only be understood within the context of the larger whole. In this way, the relationship between the parts and the whole was reversed. In the systemic approach, the properties of the parts can only be understood from the organization of the whole. As a result, systemic thinking focuses not on basic building blocks, but on basic organisational principles. Systemic thinking is "contextual", which is the opposite of analytical thinking. Analysis means to isolate something in order to understand it; systemic thinking means to put it in the context of a wider whole.[30]

The sensitive elements of biodiversity are now understood from a vision of evolution that is no longer:

> ...] the result of random mutations and natural selection [...] for we are beginning to recognize the creative unfolding of life in ever-increasing forms of diversity and complexity as an inherent characteristic of all living systems. Although mutation and natural selection are still recognized as important aspects of biological evolution, the central focus is on creativity, on the constant advance of life towards novelty.[31]

In view of this, ecosystems in different regions of the planet are unique and hardly comparable; their complexity does not allow one to think in terms of quantities

---

[30]CAPRA, Fritjof. *The web of life*: a new scientific understanding of living systems. São Paulo: Cultrix.   cap.1,   p.   20.   Available   at: <http://www.communita.com.br/assets/teiadavidafritjofcapra.pdf>. Accessed on: 08 Jun. 2019.
[31]*Ibid*, p. 165.

or in parts; what is appropriate for one area or region may not be for another, since the response of nature to human action is not yet sufficiently known, or what the amount of reversible human interference would be, in order to prevent an entire ecosystem from collapsing.

On the other hand, it is incalculable how much nations have been putting into repairing environmental degradation and the profound shake-up to which these systems are exposed, without counting all the costs related to the necessary protection and prevention measures[32].

If the economic value of biodiversity is only to consider the natural resources extracted from the environment, surely the exponential value of biodiversity as a space of relationships between species is being ignored, including here the human species and transformed nature, which in fact covers the entire world economy.

The consequences of this immoderate human interference with life can be seen in the last report published by the United Nations in 2019, which brought a sad conclusion to what planet Earth has been suffering. The report points out that 1 million species belonging to Fauna and Flora face extinction as a result of 5 important factors, such as: "changes in the use of land and sea; direct exploitation of organisms; climate change, pollution and invasion of foreign species[33].

The report also pointed out the risk for the flora, the issue of not protecting "wild plants", that is, plants that carry wild genes that are resistant to climate change, to pests, in short, that enable a plant to be resistant to some natural threat and that often when "domesticated" are lost, showing the importance of protecting this genetic natural reserve[34]. If no action is taken, food crops for humanity will be threatened with irreversible collapse.

It seems undeniable that both Fauna, Flora, and the human being are interconnected, as species living in the same "web of life".

---

[32]BRAZIL. Ministry of Environment. *Precautionary Principle.* Available at: <https://www.mma.gov.br/clima/protecao-da-camada-de-ozonio/item/7512>. Access on: 26 Oct. 2019.
[33]ORGANIZATION OF THE UNITED NATIONS - UN. *UN report shows that 1 million species of animals and plants face extinction risk.* United Nations Brazil, 08 May 2019. Available at: <https://nacoesunidas.org/relatorio-da-onu-mostra-que-1-milhao-de-especies-de-animais-e-plantas-enfrentam-risco-de-extincao/>. Access on: 06 Jun. 2019.
[34]*Ibid.*

From this perception, the International Society and individual countries have built an international and national legislative framework to protect and safeguard nature.

The next chapter will address the international tutelage and the Brazilian national legislation on the protection of Fauna and Flora, interconnected and interdependent.

3. PROTECTION OF BIODIVERSITY

The International Society organises its joint efforts on the basis of agreements between its Subjects (States and International Organisations) that are intended to produce legal effects. Such agreements are generally referred to as Treaties, although they may have numerous names[35].

A treaty is basically the reference for a protocol agreement between States or between States and International Organizations or between International Organizations themselves, regulated by international law. The terminology for this documentation is practically varied and may include the expressions: declaration, treaty, agreement, convention, letter, pact, act, among others. The treaty is a formal agreement, with well-defined delimitations that stipulate its form[36].

Environmental issues do not escape this logic and, from the growing concern with the effects of human activity on the planet, what is now called International Environmental Law is beginning to be developed.

Until 1972, in the run-up to the United Nations Conference on the Human Environment, known as the Stockholm Conference, International Environmental Law was based on intellectual and environmental movements, running in parallel with civil rights demonstrations[37].

The need for ecological awareness and a broader vision in the defense and promotion of human rights and life meets the conditions that lay the foundations for Environmental Law. The 20 years that have passed between the Stockholm Conferences and the United Nations Conference on Environment and Development (Rio92) can be considered a second phase, as the period accumulates a repertoire of multilateral agreements and studies on the subject. The third phase has as a reference

---

[35]REZEK, José Francisco. The International Treaty. *In:* REZEK, José Francisco. *Public International Law*: Elementary Course. 12. ed. São Paulo: Saraiva, 2010, cap. 1, p. 24. Available at: <https://forumdeconcursos.com/wp-content/uploads/wpforo/attachments/3992/110-DireitoInternacional-Pblico-Francisco-Rezek-15-ed-ed-Saraiva-2014-1.pdf>. Accessed on: 26 Oct. 2019.
[36]*Ibid*, p. 25.
[37]ORGANIZATION OF THE UNITED NATIONS - UN. *The UN and the Environment*. Available at: <https://nacoesunidas.org/acao/meio-ambiente/>. Accessed on: 26 Oct. 2019.

the United Nations Conference on Sustainable Development, held in Johannesburg (2002) until the present day, including the United Nations Conference on Sustainable Development held in Rio de Janeiro in 2012[38].

> [...]In the contemporary phase of international environmental law, it is increasingly based on scientific studies that show, for example, that global environmental changes are phenomena resulting from the growth of the human population and the development model that prevails on the planet: based on predatory exploitation of natural resources, uncontrolled industrialization, the immediate search for economic growth and the use of fossil fuels.[39]

Therefore, an assessment of the international legislative framework for biodiversity protection should be made.

3.1. INTERNATIONAL LEGISLATION

In 1972 in Stockholm and 1992 in Rio de Janeiro, the United Nations met to discuss solutions to global environmental problems. In addition to these, as noted, two other meetings took place in 2002 (Johannesburg) and 2012 (Rio de Janeiro), both called Conferences on Sustainable Development. However, the research will make a time cut, covering the first two, as they are enough to register the international legislation in force related to fauna and biodiversity.

The meeting of government and civil society leaders held in Stockholm from 5 to 16 June 1972, known as the United Nations Conference on the Human Environment, produced a Declaration called the Stockholm Declaration[40].

---

[38]SACHS, Ignacyet al. Sustainable development: from concept to action, from Stockholm to Johannesburg. In: SACHS, Ignacyet al. International Environment Protection. Brasilia: Unitar, Uniceub and UNB, 2009, p. 27-33. Available at: <http://www.santoandre.sp.gov.br/biblioteca/pesquisa/ebooks/372222.PDF>. Accessed on: 26 Oct. 2019.

[39]FONSECA, Fúlvio Eduardo. The convergence between environmental protection and the protection of the human person in the scope of International Law. Rio de Janeiro: Revista Brasileira de Política Internacional, v. 50, n. 1, 2007. Available at: <http://www.scielo.br/pdf/rbpi/v50n1/a07v50n1.pdf>. Accessed on: 05 Jul. 2019.

[40]ORGANIZATION OF THE UNITED NATIONS - UN. Declaration of June 5, 1972. Declaration of the UN Conference on the Human Environment. Stockholm, 1982. Available at: <http://www.direitoshumanos.usp.br/index.php/meio-ambiente/declaracao-de-estocolmo-sobre-o-ambiente-humano.html>. Accessed on: 07 Jun. 2019.

In its Preamble, it states that the UN "[...] is mindful of the need for common criteria and principles that will offer the peoples of the world inspiration and guidance to preserve and improve the human environment[41]. The objective was to call upon the peoples to universalize guiding principles for environmental protection, based on cooperation among nations, in order to minimize the impact of human action on long-term development.

The historical context reflected in the final document of the leader's meeting became the platform for evolving the issue in the environmental area, since, from it, a series of issues continued to influence and stimulate international relations, contributing to a remarkable radical change after the famous conference.

One of the main results of the Conference was the creation of UNEP - United Nations Environment Programme[42] to coordinate international environmental protection actions. Today it counts, among its partners, with other UN entities, international organizations, organizations linked to national governments and NGOs.

In addition, the Convention on International Trade in Endangered Species of Wild Fauna and Flora was signed in 1973 in Washington, and due to its relationship with the subject of this study, it will be the subject of a specific item below. As previously highlighted, there was a pressing need for change in the paradigms of development of nations. This equation would only be treated 20 years later with another important milestone for the implementation of Environmental Law: the United Nations Conference on Environment and Development, in Rio de Janeiro, from June 3 to 14, 1992[43].

The main outcomes of Rio92 were: the Rio Declaration; the Convention on Climate Change and Biodiversity Conversion; the Forest Principles; Agenda 21; other initiatives; and the definition of the institutional and financial aspects for the management of the RIO 92 Program.

---

[41]ORGANIZATION OF THE UNITED NATIONS - UN. *Declaration of June 5, 1972*. Declaration of the UN Conference on the Human Environment. Stockholm, 1982. Available at: <http://www.direitoshumanos.usp.br/index.php/meio-ambiente/declaracao-de-estocolmo-sobre-o-ambiente-humano.html>. Accessed on: 07 Jun. 2019.
[42]*Id. Environment Programme.* Available at: <https://www.unenvironment.org/>. Access on: 25 Oct. 2019.
[43]*Id. Conferences on Environment and Sustainable Development*: a mini UN. United Nations Brazil, 11 May 2017. Available at: <https://nacoesunidas.org/conferencias-de-meio-ambiente-e-desenvolvimento-sustentavel-miniguia-da-onu/>. Accessed on: 08 Jun. 2019.

The Rio Declaration, in its Principle 1, states that "[o]n human beings are at the heart of sustainable development concerns. They have a right to a healthy and productive life, in harmony with nature"[44]. And in its Principle 3 it highlights that "[o]n the right to development must be exercised so as to enable the needs of present and future generations to be met equitably," reaffirming Sustainable Development as a human right.

As for the other results, the one that will be analysed is the Convention on Biological Diversity.

3.1.1 Convention on Biological Diversity - CBD

The background to the Convention on Biodiversity, signed during the United Nations Conference on Environment and Development, suggests that it may be the first treaty that faces challenges that the previous ones have only touched upon, such as the challenges of equitable distribution of natural resources and combating biopiracy. This last concept emerges in Rio 92 and deals with the illegitimate appropriation of genetic resources and therapeutic knowledge of the countries' fauna and flora by large pharmaceutical laboratories. The active principles are internationally patented without the country of origin having any economic participation in their discovery or trade.

First, it must be noted that the Convention, ratified by Brazil on March 16, 1998 by Decree No. 2,519[45], considers the conservation of biodiversity a human concern (Preamble) and its resources subject to the sovereignty of the country where they occur (Preamble and art. 15.1)

The Convention on Biological Diversity and its sustainability equitably promotes the sharing of the benefits generated from these resources:

---

[44]ORGANIZATION OF THE UNITED NATIONS - UN. *Declaration on Environment and Development*. 1992. Prepared by the United Nations Conference on Environment and Development. Available at: <http://www.dhnet.org.br/direitos/sip/onu/bmestar/rio92.htm>. Accessed on: 25 Oct. 2019.
[45]BRAZIL. *Decree No. 2519 of March 16, 1998*. The Convention on Biological Diversity. Brasília, DF, 1998. Available at: <http://www.planalto.gov.br/ccivil_03/decreto/D2519.htm>. Access at: 27 Oct. 2019.

> [...] conservation of biological diversity, the sustainable use of its components, and the fair and equitable sharing of the benefits arising out of the utilisation of genetic resources, including through adequate access to genetic resources and appropriate transfer of relevant technologies, taking into account all rights to such resources and technologies, and through adequate funding.[46]

Article 2 of the CBD clarifies the meaning of expressions important for the understanding of the protection of biological diversity, starting by defining it:

> Biological diversity' means the variability of living organisms from all sources, comprising, among others, terrestrial, marine and other aquatic ecosystems and the ecological complexes of which they are part; also comprising diversity within species, between species and of ecosystems.[47]

Another very important concept for this research is *in situ* conservation, which would be:

> [...] the conservation of ecosystems and natural habitats and the maintenance and recovery of viable populations of species in their natural surroundings and, in the case of domesticated or cultivated species, in environments where they have developed their characteristic properties.[48]

This form of conservation is nothing more than that which protects the species in their natural place, where they naturally developed and are maintained. In short, conserving their place of origin and their qualities, it directly protects the species. This concept is closely related to the concept of "protected area", which is "a geographically defined area that is destined, or regulated, and managed to achieve specific conservation objectives", the definition of which is fundamental to ensure the protection of biodiversity.

Especially relevant for the present research is the fact that these areas, fundamental for the conservation of natural life, are those where occurrences of

---

[46]ORGANIZATION OF THE UNITED NATIONS - UN. *Convention on Biological Diversity.* United Nations, 1992, art. 1. Available at <http://www.mma.gov.br/estruturas/sbf_dpg/_arquivos/cdbport.pdf>. Access on: 07 Mar. 2019.
[47]*Ibid.*
[48]*Ibid.*

capture of animals for illegal trade are mainly recorded, which highlights the importance of an efficient inspection system.

It is also important to record the concept of "sustainable use", which is a prerequisite for conservation:

> [...] means using components of biological diversity in such a way and at such a pace that they do not lead, in the long term, to a decrease in biological diversity, thus maintaining its potential to meet the needs and aspirations of present and future generations.[49]

Also in its Article 8, the Convention brings a series of measures to be followed so that Brazil can achieve a quantitatively satisfactory conservation. The importance of determining protected areas, restoring degraded areas, elaborating guidelines for the establishment of protected areas or areas that should be protected due to their great diversity, among others, is highlighted.

The Convention seeks to raise awareness, strengthen and complement existing international instruments for the maintenance of biodiversity, once it was established as an important space for discussions on biodiversity,[50]signed by 175 countries and counting, today, with 196 countries[51].

3.1.2. Convention on International Trade in Endangered Species of Wild Fauna and Flora - CITES

The *Convention* on International *Trade in Endangered* Species of *Wild Fauna and Flora (CITES)* was signed in 1973 in Washington and aims to protect certain species from uncontrolled exploitation[52].

---

[49]AUGUST, Elmano. *ICMBIO's actions strengthen conservation.* 2013. Available at: <http://www.icmbio.gov.br/portal/ultimas-noticias/20-geral/3993-hoje-e-dia-mundial-dabiodiversidade>. Accessed on: 04 jun. 2019.

[50]*Ibid.*

[51]CONVENTION ON BIOLOGICAL DIVERSITY: *ListofParties.* Available at: <https://www.cbd.int/information/parties.shtml>. Accessed on: 25 Oct. 2019.

[52]PAULO, Government of the State of São Paulo. *Convention on International Trade in Endangered Species of Wild Fauna and Flora (CITES):* Volume IV. Available at: <http://www.terrabrasilis.org.br/ecotecadigital/pdf/convencao-sobre-o-comercio-internacional-das-especies-da-fauna-e-flora-selvagens-em-perigo-de-extincao-cites.pdf>. Access on: 25 Oct. 2019.

Ratified by Brazil in 1975 (Legislative Decree n° 54), it recognizes, in its Preamble, that "wild fauna and flora constitute in its numerous, beautiful and varied forms an irreplaceable element of the natural systems of the earth that must be protected by the present and future generations", affirming the awareness "of the growing value, of the aesthetic, scientific, cultural, recreational and **economic** points of view of wild fauna and flora"[53] (emphasis added).

It is exactly this economic value that is at the origin of the illegal capture and trading of specimens of fauna, often classified as "endangered". In this sense, the Convention establishes, in its Article II, 3 Annexes, namely:Annex I, which includes all endangered species that are or may be affected by the trade; Annex II, which includes:

> a) all species which, although not currently necessarily in danger of extinction, may be subject to this situation unless trade in specimens of such species is subject to strict regulation in order to prevent exploitation incompatible with their survival; and b) other species that need to be regulated in order to permit effective control of trade in specimens of certain species referred to in subparagraph (a) of this paragraph.[54]

Annex III, which includes:

> [...]all species which either Party declares to be subject, within the limits of its competence, to regulations to prevent or restrict their exploitation and which require the cooperation of the other Parties in the control of trade.[55]

The Parties hereby undertake not to allow trade in specimens of species listed in the Appendices, except in the cases authorized by the Convention and which relate to scientific studies, pending authorisation from the authorities of the country of origin. It also establishes the obligation of Parties to send biennial reports to the Secretariat of the treaty on measures aimed at implementing its provisions (art. VIII, 7, b).

It is known that the international illegal trade in wild animals is one of the most significant financial movements. The data on this exploitation - which will be analyzed

---

[53]BRAZIL. *Decree No. 54, 1975*. Brasília/DF, 1975. Available at: <http://www.ibama.gov.br/phocadownload/cites/legislacao/convencao_citesconf1115.pdf>. Access on: 04 jun. 2019.
[54]*Ibid.*
[55]*Ibid.*

below - demonstrate the predatory human capacity to lead some species to extinction. In any case, it is necessary to remember the commitment to preserve these resources for present and future generations.

Such initiatives require an effort of international cooperation because it is an issue that crosses the borders between countries; therefore, the document is considered an apparatus of international law with a view to reconciling development and sustainability, making explicit the regulation and control of commercialization of species.

As regards licences and certificates, the document sets out in Article VI thereof that

> 1. Licences and certificates issued in accordance with the provisions of Articles III, IV and V shall comply with the provisions of this Article. (2) Each export licence shall contain the information specified in the model set out in Annex IV and may only be used for export within a period of six months from the date of shipment. (3) Each permit or certificate shall bear the title of this Convention, the name and identification stamp of the management authority issuing it and an affixed control number assigned by the management authority. (4) All copies of a permit or certificate issued by a management authority shall be clearly marked as copies only, and no copy may be used in place of the original unless otherwise stipulated in the copy. (5) A separate permit or certificate shall be required for each shipment of specimens. (6) A management authority in the importing state of any specimen shall cancel and retain the export permit or re-export certificate and any corresponding import permit submitted in support of the import of that specimen. (7) Where appropriate and practicable the management authority may place a mark on any specimen to facilitate its identification. For this purpose "mark" means any indelible printing, lead seal or other appropriate means of identifying a specimen designed to make it as difficult as possible for unauthorized persons to imitate it.[56]

In addition, it is agreed in the text that permits will only be granted by scientific administrative authorities that will provide technical advice on the application for a permit for a particular species. The degrees of protection are described as protective measures to be adopted to the extent that the insertion of species according to their degree of vulnerability, as described in Article XVI, Annex III and its amendments:

---

[56]BRAZIL. *Decree   No.   54,   1975.* Brasília/DF,   1975.   Available   at: <http://www.ibama.gov.br/phocadownload/cites/legislacao/convencao_citesconf1115.pdf>. Access on: 04 jun. 2019.

Any Party may, at any time, send to the Secretariat a list of species which it identifies as being subject to regulation within its jurisdiction for the purpose mentioned in paragraph 3 of Article II. The names of the Parties that have submitted them for inclusion, the scientific names of each species so submitted, and any Party or derivative of the respective animals or plants specified with reference to that species for the purposes of sub-paragraph (b) of Article I, shall be included in Annex III. The Secretariat shall communicate to the Parties, as soon as possible after receipt, the lists submitted in accordance with the provisions of paragraph 1 of this Article. The list shall enter into force as part of Annex III 90 days after the date of communication of the list, any Party may, by written notification to the depository government, enter a reservation by reference to any species or part or derivative thereof. Until it withdraws such a reservation, the respective status shall be deemed to be a non-Party status of this Convention with reference to trade in the species or part or derivative thereof. (3) Any Party that submits a species for listing in Appendix III may withdraw it at any time by notification to the Secretariat, which shall communicate the withdrawal to all Parties. The withdrawal shall enter into force 30 days after the date of notification. (4) Any Party submitting a list in accordance with the provisions of paragraph 1 of this Article shall transmit to the Secretariat copies of all internal laws and regulations applicable to the protection of such species, together with such interpretations as the Party considers appropriate or as may be requested by the Secretariat. The Party shall, during the period in which the species is included in Appendix III, communicate any amendment to such laws and regulations, as well as any new interpretation, as and when adopted.[57]

From the results of the implementation of CITES in Brazil, Decree No. 3 stands out.607 of 2000, which gave practical outlines specifically for Fauna and Flora, Ordinance no. 102/98, with the purpose of regulating exotic wildlife breeding with economic and industrial purposes; Ordinance no. 118/97, which regulates Brazilian wildlife breeding, regulating trade; The commercialization is also regulated by Ordinance n° 117/97, however referring to slaughtered live animals, and by Ordinance n° 93/98, which provides on the act of import and export of live animals, of Brazilian wild and exotic fauna; the Normative Instruction n°. 02/01 of 2001, which provides for the individual identification of specimens of fauna for breeding control purposes, and Ordinance n° 113/97[58].

---

[57] Ibid.
[58] BRAZIL. Decree No. 3.607/00 of September 21, 2000. Provides on the implementation of the Convention on International Trade in Endangered Species of Wild Fauna and Flora. Available at <http://www.planalto.gov.br/ccivil_03/decreto/D3607.htm>. Access on 03 Jun. 2019.

3.2.THE NATIONAL PROTECTION

The national protection inscribed here is based prominently on public policies, as it has the capacity to organize the information from international treaties. Having an idea of these policies, identifying their impacts and results, would require more in-depth research than just a single topic.

The disorderly global growth, the consequences of which can be followed daily in the news, accuses that, in several regions of the world, entire groups of individuals are no longer having access to the minimum indispensable for their survival.

The complexity of the subject, however, is not new; the gradual degradation raises, after World War II, a perspective that refers to environmental rights as collective rights, that is, developing a notion beyond the public and private thing.

The Brazilian Civil Code of 1916, in its articles 592 and 593, illustrates well the interpretation of public and private when it refers to the environment as objects that can be exchanged. The infractions committed were considered crimes of attack against property and animals indistinctly because they attributed to the species economic values, without considering the natural set of ecosystem for human life and the preservation of the environment in general, as things of uncertain property could be subject to appropriation, as follows:

> Art. 592: Whoever is in control of something abandoned, or not yet appropriated, soon acquires the property, this occupation not being defended by law.
>
> Single paragraph. They have no ownership of the movable things again, when their own leaves them, with the intention of giving them up.
>
> Art. 593. **These are things without ownership and subject to appropriation:**
>
> I - **the wild animals, while delivered to their natural freedom**;
>
> II - the meek and domesticated that are not marked, if they have lost the habit of returning to the place where they usually retire, except the hypothesis of art. 596;
>
> III - the swarms of bees, previously appropriate, if the owner of the hive, to which they belonged, does not claim them immediately;

IV - stones, shells and other mineral, vegetable or animal substances thrown onto beaches by the sea, if they show no sign of previous dominance.59 (emphasis added)

The origin of the thinking behind the Civil Code of 1916 was based on the 19th century, whose equality, fraternity and peace emphasized the autonomy of the individual, ruling out the possibility of state intervention.

In Brazil, in the mid 1960s, the debate that constitutes Law No. 4.717/65, the Law of Popular Action, which had as its objective the protection of the individual right,60is evident. In this period it became possible to file a lawsuit to discuss a conflict pertinent to the collectivity even though it was not characterized as a procedural substitute, since it not only defended the rights of third parties, but also its own61.

It succeeds Law No. 4717/65, which debated instrumental law issues and brought to the fore themes of fundamental material law, Law No. 6 938/81, which established the National Environmental Policy and defined the subject from the chemical, physical and biological interactions responsible for life in all its forms62. The Law stood out for significant progress in the protection of human rights. In this path, Silva elucidates:

> The National Environmental Policy (PNMA) aims to regulate the various activities that involve the environment, so that there is a conscious use of environmental resources, making possible the

59BRAZIL. *Law No. 3,071 of January 1, 1916*. Civil Code of the United States of Brazil. Rio de Janeiro/DF, 1916, art. 592 and 593. Brasília, Available at: < http://www.planalto.gov.br/ccivil_03/LEIS/L3071.htm />. Access on: 06 Jun. 2019.
60Metaindividual: It is a right of indivisible nature, of which indeterminate persons are the holders, as one may seek definition in law 8.078/1990, art. 81, sole paragraph, item I (GARCIA, Gustavo Filipe Barbosa. *Indeterminate title*: Metaindividual rights are not heterogeneous. Legal Consultant, São Paulo, May 15, 2014. Available at: https://www.conjur.com.br/2014-mai-15/gustavo-garcia-direitos-metaindividuais-nao-sao-heterogeneos#top. Access on: 15 Nov. 2019).
61FIORILLO, Celso Antônio Pacheco. *Brazilian Environmental Law Course*. 14. ed. São Paulo: Saraiva, 2013. Available at: <https://forumdeconcursos.com/wpcontent/uploads/wpforo/attachments/2/1524-Curso-de-Direito-Ambiental-Brasileiro-Celso-Antonio-Pacheco-Fiorillo.pdf>. Access on: 02 jun. 2019.
62MARQUES, Vinicius Pinheiros. *Ação Popular Ambiental*: um caminho possível para a tutela jurisdicla do Meio Ambiente laboral. Lex Editora S/A, Porto Alegre. Available at: <http://www.lex.com.br/doutrina_26672823_ACAO_POPULAR_AMBIENTAL_UM_CAMINH O_POSSIVEL_PARA_A_TUTELA_JURISDICIONAL_DO_MEIO_AMBIENTE_LABORAL.as px>. Access on: 15 nov. 2019.

preservation, recovery and improvement of life giving conditions for social and economic development of the population.[63]

That said, it is necessary to analyze Law No. 7,347, published in 1985, which provides on the procedural apparatus every time, for the purpose of environmental injury or threat of injury, consumer rights, the material and immaterial artistic heritage, in addition to the aesthetic, historical, tourist and landscape aspects, it will be possible to take public civil action[64].

The following period, marked by the Constituent Assembly of 1988, accentuates the existing environmental movement and gives other contours to other civil demands, incorporates the protection of collective rights, and, among these, recognizes that there is a third kind of good: the environmental good[65].

It is in art. 225 of the Federal Constitution that the existence of an asset that is neither public nor private has been configured as an asset for common use by the people.

It follows, then, that for the first time there was an express deliberation regarding diffuse and collective interests and rights, thus harboring environmental rights in the same condition and giving these rights an indivisible nature. In other words, it is "an object that, at the same time, belongs to everyone, but no one in particular possesses it. A typical example is the atmospheric air"[66].

3.2.1 Federal Constitution

The Federal Constitution of 1988, as Silva makes clear,[67]was the first to deliberate on environmental issues. Costa Neto elucidates on this path:

---

[63]SILVA, Wesley Days of *National Environmental Policy*. JusBrasil, Cuiabá - MT, sea. 2019. Available at: <https://wesleyoperadordedireito.jusbrasil.com.br/artigos/708908402/politica-nacional-do-meio-ambiente-pnma>. Accessed on: 25 Oct. 2019.
[64]*Ibid*, p. 304.
[65]*Ibid*, p. 49.
[66]FIORILLO, Celso Antônio Pacheco. *Brazilian Environmental Law Course*. 14. ed. São Paulo: Saraiva, 2013. Available at: <https://forumdeconcursos.com/wpcontent/uploads/wpforo/attachments/2/1524-Curso-de-Direito-Ambiental-Brasileiro-Celso-Antonio-Pacheco-Fiorillo.pdf>. Access on: 02 jun. 2019.
[67]SILVA, José Afonso da. *Constitutional Environmental Law*. 4. ed. São Paulo: Malheiros, 2002.

[...] the clarification of the environmental issue came with the enactment of the so-called Citizen Constitution, focusing on the issue of the environment in a way that is related to various other values and sensitive to contemporary social demands.[68]

The theme is mentioned in several titles and chapters of the constitution. Title VIII - Of the Social Order Chapter VI, in art. 225, *caput*, assures that "everyone has the right to an ecologically balanced environment, a good for the common use of the people"[69]. Good of common use of the people can be considered to be those taken by legal determination or by their own nature. Thus, those who are used by the people, without the need for special permission, having only restrictions as to form, can be enjoyed without extrapolating and causing damage to the environment[70].

In its article 5, the FC provides for the possibility for citizens to postulate as a legitimate part of popular action aimed at annulling any acts harmful to the environment or cultural heritage[71].

Article 23, in its clauses VI and VII (regulated by Complementary Law No. 140) states[72] that the Union, States, Federal District and Municipalities have material jurisdiction:

> [...]
> VI - protecting the environment and combating pollution in all its forms;
> VII - preserving forests, fauna and flora;[73]

[68]COSTA NETO, Nicolao Dino de Castro. *Legal Protection of the Environment*. Belo Horizonte: Del Rey, 2003, p. 120-121.
[69]BRAZIL. *1988 Constitution of the Federative Republic of Brazil*. Brasília/DF, 1988. Available at: < http://www.planalto.gov.br/ccivil_03/constituicao/constituicao.htm>. Access on: 18 Nov. 2019.
[70]THE ENVIRONMENT IN THE FEDERAL CONSTITUTION OF 1988. São Paulo: Net Law, Jan. 8, 2009. Available at: <https://www.direitonet.com.br/artigos/exibir/4873/O-meio-ambiente-na-Constituicao-Federal-de-1988>. Accessed on: Jun. 05, 2019.
[71]BRAZIL. *1988 Constitution of the Federative Republic of Brazil*. Brasília/DF, 1988. Available at: < http://www.planalto.gov.br/ccivil_03/constituicao/constituicao.htm>. Access on: 18 Nov. 2019.
[72]*Id. Complementary Law No. 140, of December 8, 2011*. Brasília/DF, 09 Dec. 2011. Available at: <http://www.planalto.gov.br/ccivil_03/LEIS/LCP/Lcp140.htm>. Access on: 15 Nov. 2019.
[73]*Id. Constitution of the Federative Republic of Brazil of 1988, op. cit.*

In other words, it is the duty of the State to put into practice the commands and prerogatives provided for in the constitutional and infra-constitutional rules, through a set of concrete actions aimed at satisfying the public interest[74].

The federated entities are in charge of inspecting and applying eventual penal laws on the subject; the action of ICMBio and IBAMA, as executing agencies of PNMA, will be studied below.

Furthermore, according to Article 24 of the 1988 Magna Carta[75]:

> Art. 24 It is incumbent upon the Union, the States and the Federal District to legislate competitively on:
>
> VI - forests, hunting, fishing, fauna, nature conservation, soil and natural resources protection, environmental protection and pollution control;
>
> VII - protection of the historical, cultural, artistic, tourist and landscape heritage;
>
> VIII - liability for damage to the environment, [...].[76]

Article 225 of the Federal Constitution repeatedly assigns to the Public Power and to society in general the defense and duty to preserve the environment for present and future generations and, most importantly, translates this statement in[77]paragraph 1 :

> Paragraph 1 In order to ensure the effectiveness of this right, it is incumbent upon the Public Power:
>
> I - Preserving and restoring essential ecological processes and providing ecological management of... III - to define, in all Federation Units, territorial spaces and their components to be specially protected, being the alteration and suppression allowed only by law, forbidden any use that compromises the integrity of the attributes that justify their protection.[78]

---

[74]MONTEIRO, Natalia. *Difference between: material and legislative competence*. Available at: <____https://ntm.jusbrasil.com.br/artigos/495130395/diferenca-entre-competencia-material-e-legislativa>. Access on: 19 Nov. 2019.
[75]BRAZIL.*Constitution of the Federative Republic of Brazil 1988*, loc. cit.
[76]*Ibid.*
[77]BRAZIL. *1988 Constitution of the Federative Republic of Brazil*. Brasília/DF, 1988. Available at: <_http://www.planalto.gov.br/ccivil_03/constituicao/constituicao.htm>. Access on: 18 Nov. 2019.
[78]*Ibid.*

Historically, it was from Decree-Law No. 5,894 of October 20, 1943, that the definitive prohibition of professional hunting in the country was established. The device defined "wild fauna" and nationalized it in the aspect of ownership and control of the natural resource in order to protect it[79]. The prohibition of trade was also objectively foreseen as follows: "Article 3 - The trade of specimens of wild fauna and products and objects that involve their hunting, persecution, destruction or capture is prohibited"[80].

Finally, according to Freire, §3 of the aforementioned provision opens up possibilities of criminal sanctions for legal entities, providing that any conduct considered harmful to the environment will subject the offenders, whether natural or legal persons, to administrative and criminal sanctions, in line with the obligations to repair the damage caused[81], as will be seen in the following item in the Fauna Law.

3.2.2.Fauna Law - Law No. 5.197/67

The 1930s are marked by significant changes in the legal system, already indicating the need for protective public policies.

The Brazilian Constitution, fundamentally, is the main protection for the fauna, safeguarding in its article 225 the species of its natural purpose.

Until 1934 the hunts were not considered illegal, with the exception of the origin of the animal, if it was in a protected area. The animal without owner constituted *res nullius*, in the same meaning of the Roman law of property[82].

Law 5197, on the protection of fauna, defines more specifically what these animals are, the threat and the risk of extinction. This law hindered professional hunting

---

[79]NASSARO, Adilson Luis Franco. The evolution of the normative apparatus for the protection of fauna in the face of hunting acts in Brazil. *Historical Times*, Assisi, v. 15, p.14-30, 2011. Available at: <http://e-revista.unioeste.br/index.php/temposhistoricos/article/download/7190/5296?>. Access on: 15 nov. 2019.
[80]BRAZIL. *Law No. 5,197, January 3, 1967*. Provides on the protection of fauna and makes other provisions. Brasília, 1967. Available at: <http://www.planalto.gov.br/ccivil_03/leis/L5197.htm>. Access on: 05 mar. 2019.
[81]FREIRE, William. *Brazilian Environmental Law with updated environmental legislation*. Rio de Janeiro: AIDE, 2000.
[82]NASSARO, Adilson Luis Franco. The evolution of the normative apparatus for the protection of fauna in the face of hunting acts in Brazil. *Historical Times*, Assisi, v. 15, p.14-30, 2011. Available at: <http://e-revista.unioeste.br/index.php/temposhistoricos/article/download/7190/5296?>. Access on: 15 nov. 2019.

as a sport and trade without regulation, but also contributed to other practices - such as amateur hunting. It provides, among other things, that scientists are allowed to take samples as long as they also have a special license and are linked to research bodies or other official institutions (art. 14). Veto the export of the so-called byproducts such as non-industrialized skin and hide (Art.18).

When legislation considered wildlife as state property, it awakened to the most modern concept of sustainability. The legal treatment of flora and fauna whose holders are indeterminate - as opposed to the former res nullius, now characterizes the diffuse interest in recognition in the ecosystem, instead of its value, individual and economic.

Subsequently, the Federal Constitution of 1988 itself established the diffuse aspect of the environment as a common good for the use of the people. Law No. 7653/88 altered the wording of part of Law No. 597/67, criminalizing infractions against the fauna as inafiable. As for fishing, it is admitted in an artisanal way and for subsistence, for commercial purposes and the use of science. The biggest restrictions are in the piracema season and the fishing of species that need to be surrounded by special protection.

Law 9.605/98 - the Environmental Crimes Law - is decisively marked by penalties in cases of environmental crimes related to pollutants affecting flora and fauna. With this law, the country has moved towards protective strategies in public policies.

Conceptualized in the Brazilian Law No. 5.197/1967 - Fauna Protection Law, Article 1, wildlife is classified as being:

> Art. 1. Animals of any species, at any stage of their development and that live naturally outside of captivity, constituting the wild fauna, as well as their nests, shelters and natural breeding places.[83]

In its subsequent articles, the same Law prohibits persecution, destruction, hunting or harvesting, in line with the prohibition of trade in wildlife species and products and objects derived from their animals.

---

[83]BRAZIL. *Law No. 5,197, January 3, 1967.* Provides on the protection of fauna and makes other provisions. Brasília, 1967. Available at: <http://www.planalto.gov.br/ccivil_03/leis/L5197.htm>. Access on: 05 mar. 2019.

Art. 1 [...] **are state property and its use, persecution, destruction, hunting or harvesting is prohibited.**

§ Paragraph 1 If regional peculiarities include the exercise of hunting, the permission shall be established in a regulatory act of the Federal Public Power.

§ 2 The use, pursuit, hunting or harvesting of wildlife species on privately owned land, even when permitted in the form of the preceding paragraph, may also be prohibited by the respective owners, who shall assume responsibility for supervising their fields. In these areas, for the practice of the act of hunting, the express or tacit consent of the owners is required, under the terms of articles 594, 595, 596, 597 and 598 of the Civil Code.

Art. 2 **Professional hunting is prohibited.**

Art. 3. **The trade of specimens of wild fauna and of products and objects involved in their hunting, pursuit, destruction or harvesting is prohibited.**

§ 1. Specimens from legalised sources are excepted.

§ 2 The taking of eggs, ploughs and younglings intended for the above establishments and the destruction of wild animals considered to be harmful to agriculture or public health shall be permitted subject to a licence from the competent authority.

§ 3° The simple lack of monitoring of proof of origin of skins or other wild animal products, in land, river, sea or air shipments, which start or transit through the country, shall immediately characterize the noncompliance with the provisions of the caput of this article.[84] (Our Griffon)

After reading the respective articles of the law, the regulations and prohibitions already mentioned through trade and professional hunting are remarkable, as well as their destruction in the development stage, and stating that all specimens are property of the Brazilian State.

3.2.3 The National Environmental Policy - Law No. 6,938/81

Since 1991, with the United Nations Conference on Environment and Development, five documents have been signed that directly or indirectly relate to the protection and conservation of biodiversity at the global level. These are the five documents: Convention on Biodiversity (CBD); Convention on Climate Change;

---

[84]BRAZIL. *Law No. 5,197, January 3, 1967*. Provides on the protection of fauna and makes other provisions. Brasília, 1967. Available at: <http://www.planalto.gov.br/ccivil_03/leis/l 5197 htm>. Access on: 05 mar. 2019.

Agenda 21; Principles for Sustainable Forest Management; Rio Declaration on Environment and Development.

All these documents and events, which occurred in 1992, were based on the same environmental protection, each with its own objective; all concerned not only with the environment in itself, but also with the negative consequences that would not be preserved for the human species.

The National Environmental Policy is elaborated, its protective basis carries the same desires, that of protecting animal and plant life, as well as bringing a quality of life to man, since directly and indirectly, the negative consequences of degradation affect man. For as already analyzed in the previous chapter, both organisms are connected.

Below, the list of national instruments referring to Law 6,938/1981:

I - the establishment of environmental quality standards;

II - environmental zoning;

III - environmental impact assessment;

IV - the licensing and review of actual or potentially polluting activities;

V - incentives for the production and installation of equipment and the creation or absorption of technology, aimed at improving environmental quality;

VI - the creation of ecological reserves and stations, areas of environmental protection and those of relevant ecological interest, by the Federal, State and Municipal Public Authorities;

VI - the creation of territorial spaces specially protected by the Federal, State and Municipal Public Authorities, such as areas of environmental protection, of relevant ecological interest and extractive reserves;

VII - the national environmental information system;

VIII - the Federal Technical Register of Environmental Defense Activities and Instruments;

IX. - disciplinary or compensatory penalties for non-compliance with the measures necessary to preserve or correct environmental degradation.

X - the institution of the Environmental Quality Report, to be released annually by the Brazilian Institute of Environment and Renewable Natural Resources - IBAMA;

XI - the guarantee of the provision of information related to the Environment, obliging the Public Power to produce it, when non-existent;

XII - the Federal Technical Register of potentially polluting activities and/or users of environmental resources.

XIII - economic instruments, such as forest concession, environmental servitude, environmental insurance and others.[85] (Our Griffon).

Each instrument proposes different objectives in analysis of some incisors that call attention. It is verified:

"I - The establishment of Environmental Quality Standards", aims to establish the maximum limit before it causes damage to the environment.

"III - Environmental Impact Assessment (EIA)", in Brazil the analysis of environmental impacts began in 1981, with the publication of Law 6.938/1981 (National Environmental Policy). A requirement of foreign financial agencies to approve loans for government projects.

"IV - Licensing and review of activities that effectively or potentially pollute", aims at minimizing the environmental impacts derived from enterprises or activities that may cause environmental harm.

"VI - Creation of protected environmental spaces", provides for territorial spaces protected by the Federal, State and Municipal public entities in order to implement this law.[86] (emphasis added).

You must also bring on screen the objectives of this law below:

Article 4 - The National Environmental Policy will aim:

I - the compatibility of economic and social development with the preservation of environmental quality and ecological balance;

II - the definition of priority areas for government action regarding quality and ecological balance, taking into account the interests of the Union, the States, the Federal District, the Territories and the Municipalities

III - the establishment of environmental quality criteria and standards and norms regarding the use and management of environmental resources;

IV - the development of national research and technologies oriented to the rational use of environmental resources;

V - the dissemination of environmental management technologies, the dissemination of environmental data and information and the formation

---

[85]BRAZIL. *Law No. 6,938, of August 31, 1981.* Provides on the National Environmental Policy, its purposes and mechanisms of formulation and application, and makes other provisions. Brasília/DF, 1981. Available at: <http://www.planalto.gov.br/ccivil_03/Leis/L6938.htm>. Access on: 06 mar. 2019.
[86]RIBAMAR JUNIOR. *Main instruments of Brazilian environmental protection.* LogicAmbiental, 18 Oct. 2015. Available at: <https://www.logicambiental.com.br/protecao-ambiental/>. Accessed on: 04 Jun. 2019.

of public awareness of the need to preserve environmental quality and ecological balance;

VI - the preservation and restoration of environmental resources with a view to their rational use and permanent availability, contributing to the maintenance of an ecological balance conducive to life;

VII - the imposition, on the polluter and the predator, of the obligation to recover and/or indemnify the damages caused and, on the user, of the contribution for the use of environmental resources for economic purposes.

Article 5 - The guidelines of the National Environmental Policy shall be formulated in rules and plans, intended to guide the action of the Governments of the Union, the States, the Federal District, the Territories and the Cities in what relates to the preservation of environmental quality and maintenance of ecological balance, observing the principles established in Article 2 of this Law.

Sole Paragraph - Public or private business activities shall be carried out in accordance with the guidelines of the National Environmental Policy.[87] (Our Griffon)

It should be noted that the Convention's recommendations for member countries to devote themselves to internal policies on biodiversity and that these should be integrated with other public policies, take place in the Brazilian system. In order to follow the principles determined, countries should promote legal adjustments, implement protection mechanisms, expand a knowledge base and fund research on biodiversity.

Brazil, the signatory, has sought to comply and adopt the measures to comply with the principles that have been agreed upon. Thus, in the objectives brought about, there are forecasts for the formulation of plans and norms for all federative entities.

As regards the formation of the legal and normative framework that comprises the country's natural resources, it began under President Vargas and did not receive conceptual changes until the military dictatorship. During this period there was a regulation of natural resources; however, with a focus on economic development.

However, in the early 1980s, Law 6938/81 created the National Environmental System (SISNAMA, Law 6938/81, Article 6, which will be the object of further study when analyzing the institutional organization to combat trafficking), consisting of

---

[87]BRAZIL. *Law No. 6,938, of August 31, 1981.* Provides on the National Environmental Policy, its purposes and mechanisms of formulation and application, and makes other provisions. Brasília/DF, 1981. Available at: <http://www.planalto.gov.br/ccivil_03/Leis/L6938.htm>. Access on: 06 mar. 2019.

CONAMA - National Council of the Environment, MMA - Ministry of the Environment, IBAMA - Brazilian Institute of Environment and Renewable Natural Resources and federal, sectoral, state and municipal public administration agencies of the environment. The first two organs of the system were responsible for policy formulation and inter-institutional articulation, and the others for the execution of the National Environmental Policy[88].

The system provides for decentralised implementation, with distribution of responsibilities between the three spheres of government and participation by society.

The Federal Constitution of 1988, in its article 23, as seen, set out the conditions for the decentralization of policy formulation, giving states and municipalities that took a proactive position in environmental matters, whether local or regional. Then, the elaboration of policies more adequate to the economic and institutional reality of each federative unit is initiated, allowing a greater integration between the diverse spheres of government and the economic agents.

It was then verified that each state of the Brazilian federation adopted in its constitution the guidelines of the sparse legislations and also foreseen in the federal constitution, instruments that allowed its citizens more information about the environmental protection, as well as brought the other entities closer for this purpose, so that the municipalities also copied and were inspired by these rules[89].

3.2.4 National Biodiversity Policy - Decree n° 4.339/02

The National Biodiversity Policy is elaborated under all this legislative-influencing baggage, because with such a protective base, it would also carry the desires, the protections to the animal and plant lives, etc., all the biodiversity necessary to enable the environmental system balance.

---

[88]BRAZIL. Law No. 6,938, of August 31, 1981. Provides on the National Environmental Policy, its purposes and mechanisms of formulation and application, and makes other provisions. Brasília/DF, 1981. Available at: <http://www.planalto.gov.br/ccivil_03/Leis/L6938.htm>. Access on: 06 mar. 2019.
[89]MACHADO, Paulo Affonso Leme. Brazilian Environmental Law. 21. ed. Brasil: Cicacor, 2013. Available at: <http://licenciadorambiental.com.br/wp-content/uploads/2018/05/MACHADO-Paulo-Affonso-Leme -DIREITO-AMBIENTAL-BRASILEIRO.pdf>. Accessed on: 02 jun. 2019.

The principles set out here are for the most part those laid down in the Convention on Biological Diversity and the Rio Declaration of 1992, and those laid down in the 1988 Federal Constitution.

Below, it is interesting to observe the general guidelines that guide Law n° 4,339/02:

> I - cooperation shall be established with other nations directly or, where necessary, through agreements and competent international organizations, with respect to areas beyond national jurisdiction, in particular in border areas, Antarctica, the high seas and the great seabed, and in relation to migratory species, and other matters of mutual interest, for the conservation and sustainable use of biological diversity;
>
> II - the national effort for the conservation and sustainable use of biological diversity must be integrated into relevant sectoral or intersectoral plans, programmes and policies in a complementary and harmonious manner;
>
> III - substantial investments are needed to conserve biological diversity, which will consequently result in environmental, economic and social benefits;
>
> **IV - it is vital to predict, prevent and combat at source the causes of the significant reduction or loss of biological diversity;**
>
> **V - the sustainability of the use of components of biodiversity should be determined from an economic, social and environmental perspective, especially with regard to the maintenance of biodiversity;**
>
> VI - ecosystem management should be decentralized to the appropriate level and ecosystem managers should consider the current and potential effects of their activities on neighbouring and other ecosystems;
>
> VII - ecosystem management should be implemented at the appropriate spatial and temporal scales and long-term objectives for ecosystem management should be established, recognizing that changes are inevitable.
>
> VIII - ecosystem management should focus on structures, processes and functional relationships within ecosystems, use adaptive management practices and ensure intersectoral cooperation;
>
> IX - conditions will be created to allow access to and use of genetic resources in an environmentally sound manner by other countries that are Contracting Parties to the Convention on Biological Diversity, avoiding the imposition of restrictions contrary to the objectives of the Convention.[90] (emphasis added)

---

[90]BRAZIL. *Decree No. 4,339, of August 22, 2002.* Brasília/DF, 23 Aug. 2002. Available at: <http://www.planalto.gov.br/ccivil_03/decreto/2002/D4339.htm>. Access on: 17 Nov. 2019.

Each guideline has different objectives, but all of them guide one direction, the economic sustainability of biodiversity, since in a capitalist system to which the world is currently inserted, sustainability and preservation are thought of in this way, which is to use it without exhausting it and generate wealth.

According to the incisors listed above, IV and V, it is possible to perceive this movement of sustainability and preservation of biodiversity without losing the economic bias: "IV - it is vital to predict, prevent and fight at source the causes of the sensible reduction or loss of biological diversity", aims to establish actions to prevent and repress acts that damage biological diversity; "V - the sustainability of the use of components of biodiversity must be determined from the economic, social and environmental point of view, especially with regard to the maintenance of biodiversity", as the very incise clearly expresses in its reading, sustainability is essential for the use of biodiversity to meet economic, social and environmental needs.

Thus, after all this legislative apparatus it is possible to move towards the existing national protection system.

3.2.5 The SNUC - National System of Conservation Units - Law No. 9.985/00

The National System of Conservation Units is formed by a set of conservation units (UC) that can be federal, state and municipal. It is currently composed of twelve categories of Conservation Units, which have different objectives regarding the form of protection and permitted uses. The UCs are divided into: those that can be used in a sustainable way and preserved at the same time, and those that need more care due to their particularities and fragilities[91].

The objective of the SNUC is to enhance the role of the CUs, so that all conservation units are managed and planned in an equal and integrated manner that significantly ensures ecologically viable samples of different populations, ecosystems and habitats that suit the national territory and jurisdictional waters. Therefore, the

---

[91]BRAZIL. Ministry of Environment. *National System of Conservation Units* - SNUC. Available at: <https://www.mma.gov.br/areas-protegidas/unidades-de-conservacao/sistema-nacional-de-ucs-snuc.html>. Access on: 25 Oct. 2019.

SNUC is managed by the three spheres of government *in order to* preserve *in situ,* ensuring the conservation of ecosystems and natural habitats[92].

In addition to its administrative purpose, the SNUC has the following tasks:

- To contribute to the conservation of varieties of biological species and genetic resources in the national territory and jurisdictional waters;

- Protecting endangered species;

- To contribute to the preservation and restoration of the diversity of natural ecosystems;

- Promoting sustainable development from natural resources;

- Promote the use of nature conservation principles and practices in the development process;

- Protect natural and little altered landscapes of remarkable scenic beauty;

- To protect the relevant characteristics of geological, morphological, geomorphological, speleological, archaeological, paleontological and cultural nature;

- Recover or restore degraded ecosystems;

- Provide means and incentives for scientific research activities, studies and environmental monitoring;

- To economically and socially value biological diversity;

- To foster conditions and promote environmental education and interpretation and recreation in contact with nature; and

- To protect the natural resources necessary for the subsistence of traditional populations, respecting and valuing their knowledge and culture and promoting them socially and economically.[93]

The management of this system is divided between the following bodies: The National Environmental Council (CONAMA), a consultative and deliberative body whose function is to monitor the implementation of the SNUC; the central body represented by the Ministry of the Environment, which has the attribution of coordinator; and, finally, the executive bodies, represented in the study and municipal spheres by the local environmental agencies and in the federal sphere by IBAMA and ICMBio - Instituto Chico Mendes de Conservação da Biodiversidade, with the function

---

[92]BRAZIL. Ministry of Environment. *National System of Conservation Units* - SNUC. Available at: <https://www.mma.gov.br/areas-protegidas/unidades-de-conservacao/sistema-nacional-de-ucs-snuc.html>. Access on: 25 Oct. 2019.
[93]*Ibid.*

of implementing the SNUC, to subsidize proposals for the creation and management of conservation units[94].

3.2.6 The Environmental Crimes Law - Law No. 9605/98

Brazilian legislation does not prescribe the criminal type "Trafficking in Animals", but organizes and sanctions it in Law n° 9.605/98, in chapter V, Dos Crimes Contra O Meio Ambiente, section I, Dos Crimes Contra A Fauna, in its article 29°, which, important to point out, does not specifically punish the practice of Trafficking, but the attitudes mentioned in the following *caput:*

> **To kill, hunt, catch, use specimens of wild fauna, native or on a migratory route, without the appropriate permission, permit or authorization of the competent authority, or in disagreement with that obtained:**
>
> **Sentence - detention from six months to a year, and fine.**
>
> § 1 Incurs the **same penalties**:
>
> I - who prevents the procreation of fauna, without a license, authorization or in disagreement with that obtained;
>
> II - who modifies, damages or destroys a nest, shelter or natural crib;
>
> III - **who sells, exposes for sale, exports or acquires, keeps, has in captivity or deposit, uses or transports eggs, larvae or specimens of wild fauna, native or in migratory route, as well as products and objects from it, coming from unauthorized broodmares or without the proper permission, license or authorization from the competent authority.**
>
> § Paragraph 2 In the case of domestic guards of wild species not considered threatened with extinction, the judge may, considering the circumstances, stop applying the penalty.
>
> § 3° **Specimens of wild fauna are all those belonging to native, migratory and any other species, aquatic or terrestrial, that have all or part of their life cycle occurring within the limits of Brazilian territory, or Brazilian jurisdictional waters.**
>
> § 4 **The penalty is increased by half** if the crime is committed:
>
> I - against a rare species or considered endangered, even if only at the place of the infraction;
>
> II - during a prohibited hunting season;

---

[94]BRAZIL. Ministry of Environment. *National System of Conservation Units* - SNUC. Available at: <https://www.mma.gov.br/areas-protegidas/unidades-de-conservacao/sistema-nacional-de-ucs-snuc.html>. Access on: 25 Oct. 2019.

III - during the night;

IV - with license abuse;

V - in conservation unit;

VI - using methods or instruments capable of causing mass destruction.

§ 5° The penalty is increased up to three times if the crime is the result of professional hunting.

§ 6 The provisions of this Article shall not apply to acts of fishing.95 (Our Griffon)

Only after the advent of the Fauna Protection Law did wildlife come to be considered an asset of common use by the people, under the immediate ownership of the Union and no longer by the hunter, as provided in the Civil Code of 1916. A great rupture that meant the legislative maturation for the following decades.

It is noticeable that the legislator has conceptualized and given focus to the protection of animals, as well as everything necessary for their development that originate in the homeland, characterizing those who live here naturally, as wildlife, also highlighting the non-interference of humans in this cycle.

Coming from this protective bias and of great relevance to expose art. 32 of this law, visualizing the protection performed by the law against mistreatment directed at animals as it occurs:

Art. 32: Practice acts of abuse, mistreatment, wounding or mutilation of wild, domestic or domesticated, native or exotic animals:

Sentence - detention, from three months to a year, and fine.

§ 1 Those who carry out painful or cruel experiments on live animals, even for didactic or scientific purposes, when there are alternative resources, incur the same penalties.

§ 2 The penalty is increased by one sixth to one third if death of the animal occurs.96

The protective movement against animal violence is visible, being it in animal trafficking (object of this work) or any violence that expresses itself in any context

95BRAZIL. *Law No. 9.605, of February 12, 1998.* Provides on criminal and administrative penalties derived from conduct and activities harmful to the environment, and makes other provisions. Brasília, Available at: <http://www.planalto.gov.br/ccivil_03/leis/L9605.htm>. Access on: 06 mar. 2019.

96*Ibid.*

terminally restrained and repulsed. Having in focus of analysis the violence against the fauna, the law was foreseen and already in the very concept of fauna it is verified: "as well as its nests, shelters and natural breeding places", denoting that these words carry a protective value in favor of the animals from their primary phase until the means used for their survival.

However, where it is stated that animals of any species are state property, it does not mean the possibility of use, enjoyment or disposal of wildlife by public entities, but simply a manifestation of public domain for the purpose of protecting wild animals.

It is possible to consider that these rights have undetermined holders; even if they exist and are interconnected, there need not necessarily be a legal relationship between them. Consequently, we are talking about a situation in which the idea that only relationships between subjects of law with clearly defined obligations are legally deductible disappears.

It should be emphasized again that the ecologically harmonious environment translates a constitutional right, that is, as a fundamental right of the human person and, once the right to life is assured, the preservation of the environment is directly related to the dignity of the people, assuming a healthy life resulting from a balanced environment.

3.2.7 Government Institutions

SISNAMA - National Environmental System, foreseen in article 6 of Law 6938/81 brings to the legal world an articulated, organized and hierarchical structure, how a set of organs and entities in the Federal, State, Municipal, Territorial and Federal District spheres will be developed, besides the foundations created by the Public Power that compose it, in order to fulfill the objective of the Policy that is established in its article. 2°: "the preservation, improvement and recovery of the environmental quality propitious to life, aiming at assuring, in the Country, conditions for the socioeconomic development, the interests of the national security and the protection of the dignity of the human life"[97].

---

[97]BRAZIL. *Law No. 6,938, of August 31, 1981.* Provides on the National Environmental Policy, its purposes and mechanisms of formulation and application, and makes other provisions.

Within SISNAMA, as mentioned above, there are several other organs whose existence is worth repeating:

- CONAMA - National Council of the Environment -, a Higher Body with the function of assisting the President of the Republic in the formulation of PNMA guidelines;

- SEMA - Secretaria Especial do Meio Ambiente (Special Secretariat for the Environment), the Central Body responsible for providing, disciplining and evaluating the implementation of PNMA;

- Secretariat of the Environment of the Presidency of the Republic, a central body, whose purpose is to plan, coordinate, supervise and control, as a federal body, the government policy and guidelines set for the environment;

- IBAMA and ICMBIO - Instituto Brasileiro do Meio Ambiente e dos Recursos Naturais Renováveis and Instituto Chico Mendes de Conservação da Biodiversidade, respectively, have the purpose of implementing and enforcing the government policy and guidelines established in accordance with their respective competencies and supervision;

- The Brazilian Institute of Environment and Renewable Natural Resources - IBAMA, a federal agency with legal personality under public law, administrative and financial autonomy, linked to the Ministry of the Environment, which was created by Law No. 7,735 on February 22, 1989;

- IBAMA was born from the merger of bodies that were responsible for environmental management in the country: Special Secretary of Environment (SEMA), Superintendence of Fisheries (SUDEPE). IBAMA is a body derived from old experiences, national bodies for environmental protection[98];

- The Chico Mendes Institute of Biodiversity Conservation - Chico Mendes Institute, a federal agency with legal personality under public law, administrative and financial autonomy, linked to the Ministry of the Environment, which was created on August 28, 2007 under Law No. 11,516. It has the

Brasília/DF, 1981. Available at: <http://www.planalto.gov.br/ccivil_03/Leis/L6938.htm>. Access on: 06 mar. 2019.

[98]*Id. Law No. 7.735 of February 22, 1989.* It provides for the extinction of an agency and of an autarchic entity, creates the Brazilian Institute for the Environment and Renewable Natural Resources and makes other provisions. Brasília/DF, 1989. Available at: < http://www.planalto.gov.br/ccivil_03/leis/L7735.htm>. Access on: 07 Mar. 2019.

purpose of protecting the natural heritage, carrying out research programs for the protection and conservation of biological diversity, thus exercising its power of environmental police in protecting the Conservation Units[99].

They are also planned in SISNAMA:

• Sectional Bodies: are bodies or entities responsible for the execution of programs, projects and for the control and inspection of activities capable of causing environmental degradation; they are responsible for a large part of the environmental surveillance activity. Thus, each State of the Federation has to manage its environmental regulation agency according to its interests;

• Local bodies are municipal bodies or entities, responsible for the control and supervision of these activities in their respective jurisdictions. They have the power of environmental inspection, which authorizes them to apply applicable sanctions, interdict or close establishments that do not comply with legal determinations.

4. WILDLIFE TRADE

As seen previously, scientific concepts have been processed and have taken on new outlines while the environment has come to be considered an integral part of human life. From the cataloguing and classification carried out in the new world by European expeditions, biodiversity gains new documentary sources, involving several other areas of science. Before that, the resources were used by the natives of the land

[99]BRAZIL. *Law No. 11.516, of August 28, 2007.* Provides on the creation of the Chico Mendes Institute for Biodiversity Conservation - Chico Mendes Institute; amends Laws No. 7.735, of February 22, 1989, 11.284, of March 2, 2006, 9.985, of July 18, 2000, 10.410, of January 11, 2002, 11.156, of July 29, 2005, 11.357, of October 19, 2006, and 7.957, of December 20, 1989; revokes provisions of Law 8.028, of April 12, 1990, and Provisional Measure 2.216-37, of August 31, 2001; and makes other provisions. Brasília/DF, 2007. Available at: <http://www.planalto.gov.br/ccivil_03/_Ato2007-2010/2007/l ei/l 11516.htm>. Access on: 07 Mar. 2019.

for different purposes, very different from those that would follow the period of colonization.

> The wildlife has always been an important cultural element of the various indigenous Brazilian tribes. The most varied species were used for food, which included almost all mammals, birds, reptiles, amphibians and insects, as well as their eggs. From its parts (teeth, bones, claws, hides and others) instruments and tools were manufactured, used for several purposes. The animals, mainly birds, were essential for indigenous ornamentation, which used colorful feathers of any species to decorate the arrows, cocares, armbands, necklaces, earrings and several other items. Many birds, such as macaws and harpy, were captured and kept in the villages as suppliers of feathers for ornamentation. These ornaments were used by the Indians in their rituals, festivals and celebrations, and those who used the most beautiful pieces were more prestigious by the tribe.[100]

In the same direction that scientific explorers arrived in Brazil, traders of natural resources carried this heritage to Europe in an indiscriminate way; at that time, to possess specimens of the fauna and flora of the Portuguese colony was seen as a status of wealth.

Even data from the period indicate that there was a specialization of traders to deal exclusively with the search and delivery of such goods, displayed at open-air fairs or delivered on demand[101]. From this exploratory period are also the first references that are concerned with the extinction of Brazilian species; although the biodiversity was abundant, possibly did not correspond in total numbers of living beings of the same species[102].

The commercialization of wild animals became as important as the other colonial commercializations, as the colonizers advanced into the country, building new access ways and having new means to transport their products, the activities gained greater profitability.

It must be considered that the current legislation and the protection bodies play a fundamental role in the curbing of illegal acts, as well as the reports produced by

---

[100]RENCTAS. *1st National Report on Wildlife Trafficking*. Available at: <http://renctas.org.br/wpcontent/uploads/2014/02/REL_RENCTAS_pt_final.pdf>. Access on: 06 mar. 2019.
[101]*Ibid.* p. 15.
[102]BRAZIL. Ministry of Environment. *Brazilian Biodiversity*. Available at: <http://www.mma.gov.br/biodiversidade/biodiversidade-brasileira>. Access on: 11 jun. 2019.

Civil Society Organizations. The RENCTAS report is one of the examples that brings tangible objectives from a practical point of view. Its objectives are described:

> To detect the main characteristics of the illegal trade of wild fauna and its products in Brazil; to raise the main difficulties, deficiencies and problems related to the combat of the traffic of wild animals in Brazil; and to systematize the available information and generate data that can guide actions directed to the control and combat of the traffic of wild animals in Brazil.[103]

Despite all the international conventions and legislation dealing with the environment in the account of diffuse rights, the trafficking of Brazilian species has not yet reached an adequate level of protection, neither of the State nor of society.

4.1 CONCEPT

The illegal, predatory and indiscriminate trade in wildlife is what characterizes the nature of Animal Trafficking. Illegality is associated with the sanction of Federal Law no. 5,197/67, the Fauna Protection Law, by declaring that all animals of the national wildlife and their products are property of the State and can no longer be hunted, captured, traded or kept under private possession.

Before this period, however, the wildlife trade was an economic activity from which many families survived. As elucidated:

> However, no economic alternatives were given to the people who until then lived from this trade and who fell into marginality overnight. As a consequence, a clandestine trade emerged (Marques and Menegheti, 1982). The history of the Brazilian wildlife trade begins from there.[104]

[103]RENCTAS. *1st National Report on Wildlife Trafficking*. Available at: <http://renctas.org.br/wpcontent/uploads/2014/02/REL_RENCTAS_pt_final.pdf>. Access on: 06 mar. 2019.
[104]RENCTAS. *1st National Report on Wildlife Trafficking*. Available at: <http://renctas.org.br/wpcontent/uploads/2014/02/REL_RENCTAS_pt_final.pdf>. Access on: 06 mar. 2019.

This means that, with the withdrawal of this alternative, since 1967, the government has not offered another possibility of work or income generation to supply the space left by the activity, causing a contradiction in the action.

Illegal trade is the result of the need for economic subsistence, but not only that. Other factors - such as ancient cultural practices, the ease of obtaining quick financial returns, involvement in money laundering and drug trafficking - also stimulate such activity.

The networks of relationships between commercial agents are similarly multiple; although at the tips are suppliers and consumers, they are almost always supplied by a chain of intermediaries[105].

Furthermore, the trafficking of animals of our fauna is prevalently an illegal trade that involves, among other actions, the fraud of adulterated documentation or legal documentation, smuggling and other modes of operation, since, as has been seen, the trade in species is regulated by law[106].

Continuing the characterisation of animal trafficking, on capture and transport it is permissible to say that:

> The commercialization process, capture techniques, transportation and management, in general, are the same since the beginning until today, with aggravating because it is currently an illegal activity. The animals have always been treated in a disrespectful way, seen only as simple goods, used as a source of income.[107]

The lack of technical knowledge about the animals and the adequate treatment, until now, continues to be the main reason for the mortality during the transfer[108]; therefore, just like goods, the species are transported counting on a drop in profitability at the end of the journey, disregarding the animals that die on the way.

Such a situation represents a violation of a constitutional precept, as seen, which prohibits the cruel treatment of animals.

---

[105]*Ibid.* p. 28.
[106]*Ibid.* p. 25.
[107]*Ibid.*
[108]RENCTAS. *1st National Report on Wildlife Trafficking.* 2014, p. 15. Available at: <http://renctas.org.br/wpcontent/uploads/2014/02/REL_RENCTAS_pt_final.pdf>. Access on: 06 Mar. 2019.

4.2. IMPACTS ON BIODIVERSITY

Biodiversity defines one of the fundamental characteristics of environmental balance. The very diversity of life on the planet, in this conjunction, is said to be:

> Diversity offers conditions for humanity itself to adapt to changes in its physical and social environments and to have resources that meet its new demands. Thus, a considerable change in the diversity of species affects the quality of ecosystems to survive, such as absorbing pollution, maintaining soil fertility, purifying water, i.e. its ability to adapt becomes mitigated, and this directly affects the life of the human being.[109]

Using international treaties, it can be seen that the consolidation of concepts in this area of knowledge has been consuming specialists and other interested parties around the world and, among the discussions, are the changes in the environment and the unpredictable impacts that they can entail.

The proof of this is the brief historical overview of the wildlife trade. It should be remembered that the impacts on Brazilian biodiversity have their beginning configured by the arrival of the European explorer. Before that, the natural habitat between humans and animals demonstrated a balance in which profitability and trade were not conceptions associated with the way of life of the natives[110].

Years of exploration of the resources of the then Portuguese colony have generated, until today, devastating scenarios in the Brazilian landscapes. The degradation of the period produced such critical situations that, for certain biomes, there is no longer reversibility[111].

---

[109]LIMA, Gabriela Garcia Batista. The conservation of wild fauna and flora in Brazil: the issue of illegal trafficking of wild plants and animals and sustainable development. *Revista Jurídica da Presidência*, Brasília, v. 86, n. 9, p. 3. aug. 2007. Available at:<https://revistajuridica.presidencia.gov.br/index.php/saj/article/view/294/283>. Accessed on: 05 Jul. 2019.
[110]BRAZIL. Ministry of Environment. *Brazilian Biodiversity*. Available at: <http://www.mma.gov.br/biodiversidade/biodiversidade-brasileira>. Access on: 11 jun. 2019.
[111] VIRTUOSO, José Carlos. *The dynamics of power in the appropriation of common resources with cut-off in the use of water in the Urussanga River basin, under the focus of ecodevelopment principles*. Teste (Doutorado em Ciências Ambientais) - Graduate Program in Environmental Sciences of the University of Etremo Sul Catarinense - UNESC, Criciúma, 2019. Available at: < http://www.uniedu.sed.sc.gov.br/index.php/pos-graduacao/trabalhos-de-conclusao-de-bolsistas/trabalhos-de-conclusao-de-bolsistas-a-partir-de-2018/multidisciplinar/doutorado-8/988-as-dinamicas-de-poder-na-apropriacao-dos-recursos-

I quote:

> Brazil is home to 07 biomes, 49 eco-regions already classified, and incalculable ecosystems. It is the country with the largest existing biodiversity, gathers at least 70% of the planet's plant and animal species, and has the richest flora in the world, with up to 56,000 species of superior plants, already described; also sheltering, above 3,000 species of freshwater fish, 517 species of amphibians, 1,677 species of birds, 518 species of mammals, and can have up to 10 million insects.[112]

If we consider the concerns relating to animals at risk of extinction, the drastic reduction in the number of specimens of a species is a major cause of the ecological imbalance; since the number of animals of the same species becomes inexpressive, they may no longer be able to interact in the ecological chain with the other species[113].

Unlike the approach on the ecological extinction of species specified above, the approach on the extinction of species which exclusively considers the demographic data of an animal population does not capture more complex elements when it comes to impact on biodiversity.

> Usually, conservation studies and programs focus only on demographic extinctions, calculating the minimum viable population size, but do not give much importance to the ecological extinction of species. The most hunted animals in the rainforests that become ecologically extinct include the most important predators and seed dispersal/predators, which have stabilizing functions in the ecosystem. Many animal species are already ecologically extinct in rainforest areas with well-preserved vegetation.[114]

In data, the meaning of the environmental impact is thus translated:

> After the loss of habitat, the withdrawal of species for subsistence and trade, is the second biggest threat to wildlife. Based on the current rate

comuns-com-recorte-no-uso-da-agua-na-bacia-do-rio-urussanga-sob-o-enfoque-dos-principios-de-ecodesenvolvimento/file>. Access on: 18 nov. 2019.
[112]BRAZILIAN INSTITUTE OF ENVIRONMENT AND RENEWABLE NATURAL RESOURCES - IBAMA. *Brazilian Ecosystems*: study of ecological representativeness in Brazilian biomes. Available at: <http://www.ibama.gov.br/>. Accessed on: 06 Jul. 2019
[113]BRAZIL. Ministry of Environment. Chico Mendes Institute for Biodiversity Conservation - ICMBio. *Animal trafficking contributes to the extinction of species*. Available at: < http://www.icmbio.gov.br/portal/ultimas-noticias/4905-trafico-de-animais-contribui-para-extincao-de-especies>. Access on: 18 nov. 2019.
[114]RENCTAS. *1st National Report on Wildlife Trafficking*. 2014, p. 58. Available at: <http://renctas.org.br/wpcontent/uploads/2014/02/REL_RENCTAS_pt_final.pdf>. Access on: 06 Mar. 2019.

of destruction of natural environments, it has been estimated that about 0.25% of all species of organisms on the planet (that is, 5 out of every 200 known species) are extinct each year. It should be noted that populations of several species declined by an average of 40% between 1970 and 200012, so that the level of exploitation of some animals and plants is so high, and their trade, along with other factors such as habitat destruction, are capable of high levels of harm to the population of the species, and even lead to its extinction. In this respect, the relevance of the conservation of fauna and flora is due to the fact that, for many regions, including Brazil, the use of natural resources provides the basis for its economy and the guarantee of employment for its population. Activities such as the extraction of pearls, wood, rubber grease, export of pets, medicinal research and food, and their products, such as feathers and skins, for fashion.[115]

However, the exploitation of natural resources need not be seen only from a negative perspective. When it comes to development, the environment must be conserved to result in ecologically sound economic activities. Since an expressive group of the population lives off the results of natural raw materials, care for the environmental balance will reflect on the quality of life and income generation of these people[116].

In view of this problem, it is clear that global sustainability is maintained through the preservation of biodiversity, not only because of its ecological and economic implications.

Like other chains in the economy, illegal chains also have several agents acting.

The major dealer, usually European or North American, has a network of sellers in the receiving country and employs collectors and smugglers in the exporting country, who forward the animals to him.[117]

[115]LIMA, Gabriela Garcia Batista. The conservation of wild fauna and flora in Brazil: the issue of illegal trafficking of wild plants and animals and sustainable development. *Revista Jurídica da Presidência*, Brasília, v. 86, n. 9, p. 3. aug. 2007. Available at: <https://revistajuridica.presidencia.gov.br/index.php/saj/article/view/294/283>. Accessed on: 05 Jul. 2019.
[116]LIMA, Gabriela Garcia Batista. The conservation of wild fauna and flora in Brazil: the issue of illegal trafficking of wild plants and animals and sustainable development. *Revista Jurídica da Presidência*, Brasília, v. 86, n. 9, p. 3. aug. 2007, p. 04. Available at: <https://revistajuridica.presidencia.gov.br/index.php/saj/article/view/294/283>. Accessed on: 05 Jul. 2019.
[117]RENCTAS. *1st National Report on Wildlife Trafficking*. 2014, p. 15. Available at: <http://renctas.org.br/wpcontent/uploads/2014/02/REL_RENCTAS_pt_final.pdf>. Access on: 06 Mar. 2019.

In the fight against animal trafficking, the United Nations Environment Programme (UNEP) is[118] one of the world's most important protection networks[119].

> The agency's mandate is defined as being the leading global environmental authority that sets the global environmental agenda, promotes the consistent application of the environmental dimensions of sustainable development within the United Nations system, and serves as an authority for the global environment (UNEP, 2014, our translation) and its mission is to "provide leadership and encourage partnerships in caring for the environment, inspiring, informing and empowering nations and peoples to improve their quality of life without compromising that of future generations" (UNEP, 2014, our translation).[120]

The main objectives of the program include global monitoring that alerts nations and peoples to possible problems; measures are recommended that collaborate with the quality of life of populations in a way that does not " harm the environment and does not compromise natural resources and environmental services for future generations"[121].

4.3. TRAFFICKING IN NUMBERS

One of the bases of illegality is to make any estimate involved difficult. It is therefore not possible to obtain reliable figures for the overall total of species traded externally or internally. Even with the cruelty measured, the calculation of this economy, the number of people involved, the evasion, among other factors that could

---

[118]The United Nations Environment Programme (**UNEP**) was established in 1972 as an agency of the United Nations (UN) specifically focused on issues related to the environment (UN ORGANIZATION. UNEP - *United Nations Environment Programme*. Available at: < https://nacoesunidas.org/agencia/onumeioambiente/>. Access on: 19 Nov. 2019).

[119]PASCHOALETO, Angelo Rocha *et al.* United Nations Environment Programme - UNEP. *Study Guide*. SINUS 2014 - Sharing responsibilities in the promotion of justice, p. 05. Available at: http://sinus.org.br/2014/wp-content/uploads/2013/11/PNUMA-Guia-Online.pdf>. Access on 18 Nov. 2019.

[120]PASCHOALETO, Angelo Rocha *et al.* United Nations Environment Programme - UNEP. *Study Guide*. SINUS 2014 - Sharing responsibilities in the promotion of justice, p. 02. Available at: http://sinus.org.br/2014/wp-content/uploads/2013/11/PNUMA-Guia-Online.pdf>. Access on 18 Nov. 2019.

[121]*Ibid.*

expose with greater accuracy the size of the problem that the country faces, is not detailed.

There are, however, records that..:

> The traffic of wild animals reaches the highest levels of its practice in Europe and the United States of America, according to statistics extracted from "Environmental InvestigationAgency" (EIA), attesting that due mainly to the transport conditions of the trafficked animals, the great majority arrive dead at their destination. It has been said that the large trafficker controls a network in the receiving country, as said, in Europe and in the USA, agencies the transport of animals originating from countries with great diversity of specimens, using local collectors.[122]
>
> It is estimated, based on the registered trade in the USA, that each year this activity moves around the world the following numbers: primates: 25,000 - 40,000 live animals, most for biomedical research; birds: 2 - 5 million live animals; reptiles: 3 million turtles raised in captivity; 2 - 3 million other live reptiles; 10 - 15 million hooves; 10 million hides; 30 - 50 million manufactured products.[123]

Among the predilections for wild animals, birds are the most sought after; living or even dead, birds lend themselves to taking parts of their bodies like feathers, hides and eggs. Another well-known demand is the skin of reptiles such as crocodiles, snakes and lizards, used in all kinds of luxury artifacts.

Aquarium fish are sold for very high numbers all over the world. In the United States, between 340 and 500 million fish are smuggled, a financial movement that can reach around US$ 215 million per year, growing at a rate of 10% to 15% annually[124].

To access the most different regions of the country, RENCTAS, responsible for the research, identified that

> The traffickers use several means of transportation, according to each region, the most used being the land one, and there are also small

[122]SANTOS, Renata Rivelli Martins dos. Article 225 of the Federal Constitution and animal trafficking. Third most profitable illegal trade in the world. *Jus Navigandi Magazine*, Teresina, year 17, n. 3301, 15 Jul. 2012. Available at: < https://jus.com.br/artigos/22215>. Access on: 24 Jul. 2019.
[123]RENCTAS. *1st National Report on Wildlife Trafficking*. Available at: <http://renctas.org.br/wpcontent/uploads/2014/02/REL_RENCTAS_pt_final.pdf>. Access on: 06 mar. 2019.
[124]*Ibid*, p. 49.

aircrafts that transit without any kind of supervision or control, mainly in the Pantanal region[125]

At the international level the study has shown that:

> Brazil is an exporter of wild animals. According to the study cited above, in addition to Brazil, countries such as Argentina, Peru, Guyana, Venezuela, South Africa, Zaire, Tanzania, Kenya, Senegal, Cameroon, Madagascar, India, Vietnam, Malaysia, Indonesia, China and Russia are among the main exporters of both wildlife and flora.[126]

On the commercial frontier of Brazilian fauna and flora are still cited:

> Mexico, Saudi Arabia, Thailand, Taiwan, Spain, Greece, Italy, France and Belgium. Among the importing countries, they stand out: United States, Germany, Holland, Belgium, France, England, Switzerland, Greece, Bulgaria, Saudi Arabia and Japan, remembering that, among them, Holland is not one of the signatory countries of CITES.[127]

It has also been proven that the animals that cross the country or are exported have their origin in the northern, northeastern and central-western regions, with the southeastern region being the most expressive pole of distribution and marketing[128].

Very common all over Brazil are street fairs, free fairs or, as some authors call them, "fairs of the roll". The observations gathered by a Third Sector Organization indicate that it is possible to find the most varied types of wild animals in these places, being of public knowledge that the species are commercialized openly. In the investigation it was found that a large fair exhibits between 200 and 400 animals for

---

[125]RODRIGUES, Roberto Elias; OLIVEIRA, Taisa Cristina Sibinelli de; LEME, Sueli Mançanares. *Wildlife trafficking*: legal aspects, influence in the process of extinction of species and its ecological consequences. Juridical Scope, 31 Dec. 2007. Available at: <https://ambitojuridico.com.br/cadernos/direito-ambiental/trafico-de-animais-silvestres-aspectos-juridicos-influencia-no-processo-de-extincao-das-especies-e-suas-consequencias-ecologicas/>. Access on: 12 Jul. 2019.
[126]*Ibid.*
[127]RODRIGUES, Roberto Elias; OLIVEIRA, Taisa Cristina Sibinelli de; LEME, Sueli Mançanares. *Wildlife trafficking*: legal aspects, influence in the process of extinction of species and its ecological consequences. Juridical Scope, 31 Dec. 2007. Available at: <https://ambitojuridico.com.br/cadernos/direito-ambiental/trafico-de-animais-silvestres-aspectos-juridicos-influencia-no-processo-de-extincao-das-especies-e-suas-consequencias-ecologicas/>. Access on: 12 Jul. 2019.
[128]*Ibid.*

sale - in smaller fairs, between 20 and 60 animals. Once again the predilection fell on birds, representing about 95% of all animals identified[129].

Regarding the modalities of animal trafficking in Brazil, the RENCTAS-Rede Nacional de Combate ao Tráfico de Animais Silvestres report points out that there are four types of classification for this illicit activity. The classification was made according to the final destination of the species in question[130].

Private collectors and Zoo Parks occupy the first type in the classification. This is one of the most harmful actions of the commercialization network, since its priority is the species considered rare, precisely those that are on the verge of extinction. These collectors are located internationally in Europe, Asia and North America. The blue macaw (*Anodorhynchusleari*), the blue macaw (*Anodorhynchushyacinthinus*), the macaw (*Ara ararauna), the red-tailed* parrot (*Amazona brasiliensis)*, The *harpy* eagle (*Harpy* eagle), the golden lion tamarin (*Leontopithecusrosalia)* and the ocelot (*Leoparduspardalis*) are among the most valuable species for commercialization[131].

Biopiracy of species is the second classified type, the destination being specifically for scientific purposes. Biopiracy involves the extraction of chemical substances produced by animals and which will give rise to products for use in medicine, cosmetics, among others. One can consider the jaraca (*Bothrops jaraca*), the rattlesnake (*Crotalus sp.*), frogs, spiders, beetles and wasps, as species that appear in this category[132].

Animals for domestication are the ones that most influence the national traffic, and, in this third category, we find all kinds of wild animals[133].

Finally, as a fourth type of farm are the animals from which various products can be extracted. In this regard there is a variation in the predilection for species due to cultural trends linked mainly to the world of fashion. Marketing is based on hides and skins, feathers - widely used as adornment, claws and prey. Of the animals involved in this trade, we find the psitacids whose feathers are much appreciated, the *boa*

[129]*Ibid.*
[130]RENCTAS. *1st National Report on Wildlife Trafficking*. 2014, p. 17. Available at: <http://renctas.org.br/wpcontent/uploads/2014/02/REL_RENCTAS_pt_final.pdf>. Access on: 06 Mar. 2019.
[131]RENCTAS. *1st National Report on Wildlife Trafficking*. 2014, p. 17. Available at: <http://renctas.org.br/wpcontent/uploads/2014/02/REL_RENCTAS_pt_final.pdf>. Access on: 06 Mar. 2019.
[132]*Ibid*, p. 17.
[133]*Ibid*, p. 19.

constrictor (boa constrictor), the teiú lizard *(Tupinambis sp.)* and alligators *(Caiman sp.),* for hides and skins, and mammals, especially the jaguar *(Pantera onca),* the ocelot *(Leoparduspardalis) and wild* cats *(Leopardus sp.),* appreciated for the texture and pattern of their skins[134].

From this information, it can be seen that there is an important import and export market, demand where the responsibility of CITES and IBAMA is located. However, such agencies do not present a very significant number of registered traders, whether they are exporters or importers. In the 2003 update, for example, the exporters with registration at IBAMA maintained 50 spaces for rational breeding of wild animals; of these 45 were considered active, although only15 were up to date with the registrations. Of the importers, in this same year, there were 90 registrations in IBAMA's list, 46 of them working and 50 broodmares with their complete data[135].

4.4. THE FIGHT IN THE WORLD AND IN BRAZIL

Both the deliberations of international conferences and the development of Brazilian legislation on biodiversity converge to characterize this trade as illegal. Civil society, in turn, has organized itself into legal associations, producing other mechanisms to help improve the legal system and, especially, to combat the trafficking of fauna in the country.

However, the description in the reports produced by Civil Society Organisations does not present a very positive scenario for achieving a more assertive resolution. Even when the routes of wildlife trafficking, inside and outside the country, and their main commercialization points are identified, it is also perceived that the organization of traffickers changes rapidly in order to anticipate and achieve success if a situation conducive to police action is created.

---

[134]*Ibid,* p. 20.
[135]LIMA, Gabriela Garcia Batista. The conservation of wild fauna and flora in Brazil: the issue of illegal trafficking of wild plants and animals and sustainable development. *Revista Jurídica da Presidência,* Brasília, v. 86, n. 9, p. 3. aug. 2007. Available at: <https://revistajuridica.presidencia.gov.br/index.php/saj/article/view/294/283>. Accessed on: 05 Jul. 2019.

In cases of investigations conducted by the civil police, the chances of the action being more successful are usually greater than that of the environmental police, since traffickers are able to identify the movement of policemen by uniform.

Moreover, the places of illegal trade are spaces of great movement. It is exemplified that:

> Rio de Janeiro and Baixada Fluminense are the poles of illegal animal trade. At the Caxias Fair alone, at least two thousand animals are sold every Sunday. In Feira de Santana, Bahia, in the Supply Center of Feira and even in Marechal Deodoro streets and on Avenida Senhor dos Passos, located in the central region, macaws, parrots, toucans, wild cats and birds are sold and trafficked abroad. In the Amazon, the animals, besides being trafficked by air, are taken by river to the Mercado de Iquitos, in Peru, and Mercado Ver-o-Peso, in Belém, Pará.[136]

Most likely, the fairs have places for the animals to wait for the moment of exposure or even to miss a possible police action.

In fact, combating wildlife trafficking in the country has proved to be a difficult task for the authorities because several factors are related to each other and directly linked to many others. The RENCTAS report lists such problems and brings suggestions that will be addressed in the later topic.

As regards border traffic, the problems identified are: lack of customs posts; lack of contingency and training of officers; lack of adequate equipment and materials; large territorial dimension of the country; lack of exchanges with border countries; lack of international cooperation[137].

As for Internet trafficking, the problems identified are: discretion and ease of buying and selling; difficulty in identifying negotiators; lack of a specialised body to combat this type of tragedy; lack of legislation on the subject[138].

---

[136]RODRIGUES, Roberto Elias; OLIVEIRA, Taisa Cristina Sibinelli de; LEME, Sueli Mançanares. *Wildlife trafficking*: legal aspects, influence in the process of extinction of species and its ecological consequences. Juridical Scope, 31 Dec. 2007. Available at: <https://ambitojuridico.com.br/cadernos/direito-ambiental/trafico-de-animais-silvestres-aspectos-juridicos-influencia-no-processo-de-extincao-das-especies-e-suas-consequencias-ecologicas/>. Access on: 12 Jul. 2019
[137]RENCTAS. *1st National Report on Wildlife Trafficking*. 2014, p. 70. Available at: <http://renctas.org.br/wpcontent/uploads/2014/02/REL_RENCTAS_pt_final.pdf>. Access on: 06 Mar. 2019.
[138]*Ibid*, p. 71.

Regarding scientific trafficking, the problems identified are: the use, by researchers, of credentials and official authorizations granted to the institutions for which they work; indiscriminate collection and waste of faunal material; the actions of foreign companies; little control and participation of the Brazilian Government in projects developed in cooperation and/or by foreign institutions and researchers[139].

Regarding the destination of the seized animals, the problems identified are: lack of appropriate places to send the seized animals; high cost of maintenance of the Sorting Centers; overcrowding of the institutions able to receive these animals, the few Sorting Centers and zoos; lack of scientific knowledge to perform the release of these animals[140].

As for the Brazilian legislation, the problems identified are: lack of knowledge of the law by the population; lack of compliance with the law; lack of rigidity in the application of the law; little consideration for the crime against wildlife by the legal authorities[141].

Despite the reality of animal trafficking, CITES is another protective factor. The numbers recorded indicate that about 30,000 species are under monitored protection against international trade - a form of internal environmental protection to reconcile environmental preservation with sustainable development, without denying the possibility of trade through the necessary regulations[142].

Among other issues faced in analyzing the report, the Organization found that the popular names of species may indicate different animals from one region to another; for this reason, the scientific names were compared with the common names reported by state IBAMA agencies. The unidentified names were added to the category "other", such as animals of exotic fauna and others not researched[143].

Internationally, the same report considered the Amazon border region to be a problem because it borders Brazilian states with Guyana, Venezuela and Colombia.

---

[139]*Ibid,* p. 31.
[140]RENCTAS. *1st National Report on Wildlife Trafficking.* 2014, p. 72. Available at: <http://renctas.org.br/wpcontent/uploads/2014/02/REL_RENCTAS_pt_final.pdf>. Access on: 06 Mar. 2019.
[141]*Ibid.*
[142]LIMA, Gabriela Garcia Batista. The conservation of wild fauna and flora in Brazil: the issue of illegal trafficking of wild plants and animals and sustainable development. *Revista Jurídica da Presidência,* Brasília, v. 86, n. 9, p.7. aug. 2007. Available at:<https://revistajuridica.presidencia.gov.br/index.php/saj/article/view/294/283>. Accessed on: 16 Jul. 2019.
[143]RENCTAS, *op. cit.* , p. 31.

Brazilian inspection is practically non-existent given the wide extension of the Amazon region.

The main trafficking points that have been identified are in Tabatinga (BR), Leticia (CO), Manaus (AM), Rio Branco (AC), Porto Velho (RO), Bonfim (RR), Uruguaiana (RS) and Foz do Iguaçu (PR)[144].

4.5.SUGGESTIONS FOR DEALING WITH THE PROBLEM

The first concerns about the extinction of species date back to the 19th century, as commercial interests found that resources could quickly become scarce; much more consideration was given to the commercial aspect than really to the impact these interests had on biodiversity.

In the 20th century the concern of environmentalists with the possible extinction of whales became notorious. Initially   hunted for subsistence, they were raised to the condition of large commercial scale when the meat and other body parts reached great value in the international market. At the same time, WWF - an acronym for World WildlifeFund - called for an environmental protection campaign warning of the extinction of species whose panda was an example of the escalation of an announced tragedy.

In any case, the lessons learned about species preservation and combating illegal animal trafficking are associated with the determination of parameters that enable the planning of actions and strategies. With this assumption, the report of the organization RENCTAS presents the following suggestions:

- With regard to border traffic, it is suggested: the establishment of customs posts; the increase of the contingent and training of agents; the acquisition of the necessary equipment and materials; greater exchange between countries; greater international cooperation[145];

---

[144]RENCTAS. *1st National Report on Wildlife Trafficking*. 2014, p. 24. Available at: <http://renctas.org.br/wpcontent/uploads/2014/02/REL_RENCTAS_pt_final.pdf>. Access on: 06 Mar. 2019.
[145]*Ibid*, p. 70.

• In relation to Internet trafficking, it is suggested: the control and inhibition of sites that carry out this trade; the search for and permanent identification of these sites; the inclusion in environmental crime laws[146];

• In relation to the traffic in keepers of Fauna it is suggested: greater inspection and control of the keepers by the responsible organs; individual marking of the animals by means of microchips; greater rigidity in the permissions to sell the animals; differentiated treatment for keepers of endangered species listed in Appendix I of CITES[147];

• Regarding scientific trafficking, it is suggested: greater control and participation in projects and agreements in partnership with foreign researchers and institutions; greater criteria for the collection and use of faunal material; centralization of collection authorization emissions; greater care in the transfer of acquired information; better control by institutions over the collection materials of their researchers[148];

• Regarding the destination of the apprehended animals, it is suggested: resources for the construction and maintenance of Sorting Centers; development of scientific research that can generate knowledge about the area of occurrence of the species, population size, support capacity of the habitats, among many others[149];

• In relation to the Brazilian Legislation it is suggested: greater disclosure and clarification of the law; stricter application; updating of the law, providing for internet traffic[150].

---

[146]RENCTAS. *1st National Report on Wildlife Trafficking*. 2014, p. 71. Available at: <http://renctas.org.br/wpcontent/uploads/2014/02/REL_RENCTAS_pt_final.pdf>. Access on: 06 Mar. 2019.
[147]*Ibid.*
[148]*Ibid*, p. 72.
[149]*Ibid.*
[150]*Ibid.* p. 73.

5. FINAL CONSIDERATIONS

The present subject instigates the deepening of the reported information and, in light of the academic experience, offers motivation for the study of the necessary advances in the Brazilian legislation. It is important that society, as a whole that transforms the environment around it, takes a more emphatic attitude and positively transforms this reality.

As can be seen, the concept of environment is very broad and goes far beyond the natural environment. Fauna and flora, on the other hand, are more specific, having their concepts directed respectively to a group of animals belonging to natural life, free and living in a certain region and to a group of organisms of the plant kingdom present in certain places, and with peculiar characteristics of the place.

Biodiversity in its definition encompasses lives, or a vast biological diversity with exuberant amounts of living forms on Planet Earth.

The Trafficking of Wild Animals in Brazilian fauna and the associated impunity, since colonial times, causes repercussions, either in the public power, or in the specialists and scientists who mobilize around the cause, becoming the drivers of small but significant changes.

The consequences of this disproportionate human interference with life can be seen in the last report published by the United Nations in 2019, which brought a sad conclusion to what planet Earth has been suffering. The report points out that 1 million species belonging to Fauna and Flora face extinction.

Unfortunately, the presence of public authorities is still small to account for a country of continental proportions; planning, material structure and human resources are lacking. The data found in the development of this work demonstrate the need for greater consistency in order to report faithfully the values involved. By value we mean not only the economic values driven by illegality, but also those applied to the subjective value of the right to protection and life of wild animals.

In this context, the importance of international conferences and treaties is highlighted because they give quality to the discussions and provide a basis for the progressive amendment of the legislation of the signatory nations. These opportunities promote the updating of data and the exchange of information on the transit of smuggled animals between countries.

The production of reports, in particular, is a tool for the daily monitoring of endangered species. The exposure of documents is a way to publish results, put pressure on the authorities, raise awareness and educate society.

It is possible to recognize a deficit in Brazilian legislation: after all, trafficking adapts and changes rapidly to the conditions presented, while the formality of legislative doctrine requires much more time for bureaucratic processes.

Regarding International Law, the Convention on International Trade in Endangered Species of Wild Fauna and Flora, known as CITES, stands out as a treaty aimed at the protection and conservation of fauna and flora

The challenges related to this issue touch upon illegality, the preservation of fauna, social and political aspects and the fragility of the economy that can be produced by sustainable development. Wildlife trade is an activity that must be carefully monitored and regulated, taking into consideration investments and public policies that must be employed by the government for the qualification of import and export.

Economic exploitation is a proven demand for the use of fauna that can be invested through rational captive breeding and collaborate as part of maintaining ecological balance. Therefore it is necessary to consider that the natural resource is finite and animal life must be treated with the required constitutional dignity. Here it is important to clarify that the commitment to sustainable development with the improvement of people's quality of life has the same meaning as the commitment to the environment.

The main national protection comes from the Brazilian Federal Constitution of 1988, which, in accordance with international treaties and agreements, determines who are responsible for the protection of the Brazilian fauna and together establishes the competent federal entities and their attributions. Article 225 of the Constitution is an outstanding example that it is not only the State's responsibility to protect biodiversity, but also the population, thus ensuring that all human beings are guaranteed an ecologically balanced environment.

It is worth highlighting that the attention to wild animals considers these beings as participants of the diffuse rights; therefore, it focuses directly on the expansion of fundamental human rights because it improves the living space for all and increases the potential for human development.

The traffic of animals rises against all this national and international protection and haunts biodiversity with gigantic damages, bringing as the most devastating result, the extinction of the Fauna, disrespecting as already said the legal predictions but also damaging the balance relations of life, because the results go far beyond the simple withdrawal of specimens from nature.

The solutions for this problem are brought in the National Report on Wildlife Trafficking, are possible solutions: the implementation of border checkpoints; materials that help in the combat; repression on the Internet of commercialization; and the awareness of people, through the dissemination of campaigns against animal trafficking.

Finally, when considering the sum of the research presented, it becomes clear that the theme can be approached by multiple facets and that not by far has this work exhausted the cast of possible approaches. Although it is not plausible to conclude the research problem, mainly because it is a subject based on illegality, it is essential to reaffirm the commitment of the academic environment to the study of the data presented and its participation as a space for knowledge production, seeking possible solutions and reflections.

REFERENCES

BOOKS

BECHARA, Erika. *The protection of fauna from the constitutional point of view*. São Paulo: Juarez de Oliveira, 2003.

CAPRA, Fritjof. *The web of life*: a new scientific understanding of living systems. São Paulo: Cultrix. Available at: <http://www.communita.com.br/assets/teiadavi dafritjofcapra.pdf>. Access on: 08 Jun. 2019.

WORLD COMMISSION ON ENVIRONMENT AND DEVELOPMENT - CMMAD. *Our Common Future*. 2. ed. Rio de Janeiro: Fundação Getúlio Vargas, 1991.

COSTA NETO, Nicolao Dino de Castro. *Legal Protection of the Environment*. Belo Horizonte: Del Rey, 2003.

FIORILLO, Celso Antônio Pacheco. *Brazilian Environmental Law Course*. 14. ed. São Paulo: Saraiva, 2013. Available at: <https://forumdeconcursos.com/wpcontent/uploads/wpforo/attac hments/2/1524-Brazilian-Environmental-Right-Celso-Antonio-Pacheco-Fiorillo.pdf>. Access on: 02 jun. 2019.

FONSECA, Fúlvio Eduardo. THE CONVERGENCE BETWEEN ENVIRONMENTAL PROTECTION AND THE PROTECTION OF THE HUMAN PERSON UNDER INTERNATIONAL LAW. Rio de Janeiro: Revista Brasileira de Política Internacional, v. 50, n. 1, 2007. Available at: <http://www.scielo.br/pdf/rbpi/v50n1/a07v50n1.pdf>. Accessed on: 05 Jul. 2019.

MACHADO, Paulo Affonso Leme. *Brazilian Environmental Law*. 21. ed. Brasil: Cicacor, 2013. Available at: <http://licenciadorambiental.com.br/wp-content/uploads/2018/05/MACHADO-Paulo-Affonso-Leme.-DIREITO-AMBIENTAL-BRASILEIRO.pdf>. Accessed on: 02 jun. 2019.

MARQUES, Vinicius Pinheiros. *Ação Popular Ambiental*: um caminho possível para a tutela jurisdicla do Meio Ambiente laboral. Lex Editora S/A, Porto Alegre. Available at: <http://www.lex.com.br/doutrina_26672823_ACAO_POPULAR_AMBIENTAL_UM_C AMINHO_POSSIVEL_PARA_A_TUTELA_JURISDICIONAL_DO_MEIO_AMBIENTE _LABORAL.aspx>. Access on: 15 nov. 2019.

ORGANIZATION OF THE UNITED NATIONS - UN. *Brundtland Report* - Our Common Future. 2. ed. Rio de Janeiro: Fundação Getúlio Vargas, 1991. Available at: <https://edisciplinas.usp.br/pluginfile.php/4245128/mod_resource/content/3/Nosso%2 0Futuro%20Comum.pdf>. Access on: 10 nov. 2019.

REZEK, José Francisco. The International Treaty. In: REZEK, José Francisco. *Public International Law*: Elementary Course. 12. ed. São Paulo: Saraiva, 2010. Available at: https://forumdeconcursos.com/wp-content/uploads/wpforo/attachments/3992/110-DireitoInternacional-Pblico-Francisco-Rezek-15-ed-ed-Saraiva-2014-1.pdf. Accessed on: 26 Oct. 2019.

SILVA, José Afonso da. *Constitutional Environmental Law*. 4. ed. São Paulo: Malheiros, 2002.

SILVA, Wesley Days of *National Environmental Policy*. JusBrasil, Cuiabá - MT, sea. 2019.   Available   at: <https://wesleyoperadordedireito.jusbrasil.com.br/artigos/708908402/politica-nacional-do-meio-ambiente-pnma>. Accessed on: 25 Oct. 2019.

ARTICLES

ANDRADE FILHO, Álvaro Ricardo Azevedo; CALÇADO, Gustavo Silva. *Law as value*. São Paulo:Aprombh. Available at: <http://www.aprombh.com.br/artigos/1218-direito-enquanto-valor>. Accessed on: 03 jun. 2019.

BARBIERI, Edison. *Biodiversity*: the variety of life on planet Earth: Current knowledge about biodiversity. South Coast Research and Development Unit (Cananéia), of the Advanced Center for Technology Research of Marine Fisheries Agribusiness, Instituto de Pesca, Apta (Paulista Agency for Agribusiness Technology), Secretariat of Agriculture and Supply of the State of São Paulo, São Paulo, p. 1-16, 2010. Available at: <https://www.pesca.sp.gov.br/biodiversidade.pdf>. Accessed on: 04 Jun. 2019.

FRANCO, José Luiz de Andrade. The concept of biodiversity and the history of conservation biology: from wilderness preservation to biodiversity conservation. *History*, São Paulo, v. 32, 2013, p. 21-48. Available at: <http://www.scielo.br/pdf/his/v32n2/a03v32n2.pdf>. Access on: 04 jun. 2019.

GARCIA, Gustavo Filipe Barbosa. *Undetermined ownership*: Metaindividual rights are not heterogeneous. Legal Consultant, São Paulo, May 15, 2014. Available at: https://www.conjur.com.br/2014-mai-15/gustavo-garcia-direitos-metaindividuais-nao-sao-heterogeneos#top. Access on: 15 Nov. 2019.

LIMA, Gabriela Garcia Batista. The conservation of wild fauna and flora in Brazil: the issue of illegal trafficking of wild plants and animals and sustainable development. *Revista Jurídica da Presidência*, Brasília, v. 86, n. 9, p. 3. aug. 2007. Available at:<https://revistajuridica.presidencia.gov.br/index.php/saj/article/view/294/283>. Accessed on: 05 Jul. 2019.

PAULO, Government of the State of São Paulo. *Convention on International Trade in Endangered Species of Wild Fauna and Flora (CITES)*: Volume IV. Available at: <http://www.terrabrasilis.org.br/ecotecadigital/pdf/convencao-sobre-o-comercio-

internacional-das-especies-da-fauna-e-flora-selvagens-em-perigo-de-extincao-cites.pdf>. Access on: 25 Oct. 2019.

NASSARO, Adilson Luis Franco. The evolution of the normative apparatus for the protection of fauna in the face of hunting acts in Brazil. *Historical Times*, Assisi, v. 15, p.14-30, 2011. Available at: <http://e-revista.unioeste.br/index.php/temposhistoricos/article/download/7190/5296?>. Access on: 15 nov. 2019.

PASCHOALETO, Angelo Rocha et al. United Nations Environment Programme - UNEP. *Study Guide*. SINUS 2014 - Sharing responsibilities in the promotion of justice. Available at: http://sinus.org.br/2014/wp-content/uploads/2013/11/PNUMA-Guia-Online.pdf>. Access on 18 Nov. 2019.

RIBAMAR JUNIOR. *Main instruments of Brazilian environmental protection*. LogicAmbiental, 18 Oct. 2015. Available at: <https://www.logicambiental.com.br/protecao-ambiental/>. Accessed on: 04 Jun. 2019.

RODRIGUES, Roberto Elias; OLIVEIRA, Taisa Cristina Sibinelli de; LEME, Sueli Mançanares. *Wildlife trafficking*: legal aspects, influence in the process of extinction of species and its ecological consequences. Juridical Scope, 31 Dec. 2007. Available at: <https://ambitojuridico.com.br/cadernos/direito-ambiental/trafico-de-animais-silvestres-aspectos-juridicos-influencia-no-processo-de-extincao-das-especies-e-suas-consequencias-ecologicas/>. Access on: 12 Jul. 2019.

SANTOS, Renata Rivelli Martins dos. Article 225 of the Federal Constitution and animal trafficking. Third most profitable illegal trade in the world. *Jus Navigandi Magazine*, Teresina, year 17, n. 3301, 15 Jul. 2012. Available at: < https://jus.com.br/artigos/22215>. Access on: 24 Jul. 2019.

COMPLETION WORK

VIRTUOSO, José Carlos. *The dynamics of power in the appropriation of common resources with cut-off in the use of water in the Urussanga River basin, under the focus of ecodevelopment principles*. Teste (Doutorado em Ciências Ambientais) - Graduate Program in Environmental Sciences of the University of Etremo Sul Catarinense - UNESC, Criciúma, 2019. Available at: < http://www.uniedu.sed.sc.gov.br/index.php/pos-graduacao/trabalhos-de-conclusao-de-bolsistas/trabalhos-de-conclusao-de-bolsistas-a-partir-de-2018/multidisciplinar/doutorado-8/988-as-dinamicas-de-poder-na-apropriacao-dos-recursos-comuns-com-recorte-no-uso-da-agua-na-bacia-do-rio-urussanga-sob-o-enfoque-dos-principios-de-ecodesenvolvimento/file>. Access on: 18 nov. 2019.

LEGISLATION

BRAZIL. *1988 Constitution of the Federative Republic of Brazil*. Brasília/DF, 1988. Available at: <_http://www.planalto.gov.br/ccivil_03/constituicao/constituicao.htm>. Access on: 18 Nov. 2019.

_____. *Decree No. 54, 1975*. Brasília/DF, 1975. Available at: <http://www.ibama.gov.br/phocadownload/cites/legislacao/convencao_citesconf1115. pdf>. Access on: 04 jun. 2019.

_____. *Decree No. 2.519 of March 16, 1998*. The Convention on Biological Diversity. Brasília/DF, 1998. Available at: <http://www.planalto.gov.br/ccivil_03/decreto/D2519.htm>. Access on: 06 mar. 2019.

_____. *Decree No. 3.607/00 of September 21, 2000*. Provides on the implementation of the Convention on International Trade in Endangered Species of Wild Fauna and Flora. Available at <http://www.planalto.gov.br/ccivil_03/decreto/D3607.htm>. Access on 03 Jun. 2019.

BRAZIL. *Decree No. 4,339, of August 22, 2002*. Brasília/DF, 23 Aug. 2002. Available at: <http://www.planalto.gov.br/ccivil_03/decreto/2002/D4339.htm>. Access on: 17 Nov. 2019.

_____. *Law No. 3,071 of January 1, 1916*. Civil Code of the United States of Brazil. Rio de Janeiro/DF, 1916, art. 592 and 593. Brasília, Available at: < http://www.planalto.gov.br/ccivil_03/LEIS/L3071.htm />. Access on: 06 Jun. 2019.

_____. *Law No. 5,197 of January 3, 1967*. Provides on the protection of fauna and makes other provisions. Brasília, 1967. Available at: <http://www.planalto.gov.br/c civil_03/leis/L5197.htm>. Access on: 05 mar. 2019.

_____. *Law No. 6938, of August 31, 1981*. Provides on the National Environmental Policy, its purposes and mechanisms of formulation and application, and makes other provisions. Brasília/DF, 1981. Available at: <http://www.planalto.gov.br/ccivil_03/Leis/L6938.htm>. Access on: 06 mar. 2019.

_____. *Law No. 7.735 of February 22, 1989*. It provides for the extinction of an agency and of an autarchic entity, creates the Brazilian Institute for the Environment and Renewable Natural Resources and makes other provisions. Brasília/DF, 1989. Available at: < http://www.planalto.gov.br/ccivil_03/leis/L7735.htm>. Access on: 07 Mar. 2019.

_____. *Law No. 9605 of 12 February 1998*. Provides on criminal and administrative penalties derived from conduct and activities harmful to the environment, and makes other provisions. Brasília, Available at: <http://www.planalto.gov.br/ccivil_03/leis/L9605.htm>. Access on: 06 mar. 2019.

_____. *Law No. 11.516 of August 28, 2007*. Provides on the creation of the Chico Mendes Institute for Biodiversity Conservation - Chico Mendes Institute; amends Laws No. 7.735, of February 22, 1989, 11.284, of March 2, 2006, 9.985, of July 18, 2000, 10.410, of January 11, 2002, 11.156, of July 29, 2005, 11.357, of October 19, 2006, and 7.957, of December 20, 1989; revokes provisions of Law 8.028, of April 12, 1990, and Provisional Measure 2.216-37, of August 31, 2001; and makes other provisions. Brasília/DF, 2007. Available at: <http://www.planalto.gov.br/ccivil_03/_Ato2007-2010/2007/Lei/L11516.htm>. Access on: 07 Mar. 2019.

_____. *Complementary Law No. 140, of December 8, 2011*. Brasília/DF, 09 Dec. 2011. Available at: <http://www.planalto.gov.br/ccivil_03/LEIS/LCP/Lcp140.htm>. Access on: 15 Nov. 2019.

ORGANIZATION OF THE UNITED NATIONS - UN. *Declaration of June 5, 1972*. Declaration of the UN Conference on the Human Environment. Stockholm, 1982. Available at: <http://www.direitoshumanos.usp.br/index.php/meio-ambiente/declaracao-de-estocolmo-sobre-o-ambiente-humano.html>. Accessed on: 07 Jun. 2019.

WEB SITES

AUGUST, Elmano. *ICMBIO's actions strengthen conservation*. 2013. Available at: <http://www.icmbio.gov.br/portal/ultimas-noticias/20-geral/3993-hoje-e-dia-mundial-dabiodiversidade>. Accessed on: 04 jun. 2019.

BIODIVERSITY. Brazil: Uesc. Available at: <http://nead.uesc.br/arquivos/Biologia/modulo_8bl oco_1/uni_biodiversity_ecology/support_material/M8EBU1_biodiversity.pdf>. Access on: 02 jun. 2019.

CONVENTION ON BIOLOGICAL DIVERSITY: *ListofParties*. Available at:
<https://www.cbd.int/information/parties.shtml>. Accessed on: 25 Oct. 2019.

Flora is recognized as one of the most important in the world. Brazil Legacy,
Environment, Plant Species, 11 Apr. 2012. Available at:
<http://www.brasil.gov.br/noticias/meioambiente/2012/04/flora-brasileira>. Accessed
on: 04 Jun. 2019.

_____. *Red Book of the Brazilian Fauna Threatened with Extinction*. Brasília:
ICMBIO, 2018. Available at:
<http://www.icmbio.gov.br/portal/images/stories/comunicacao/publicacoes/publicacoe
s-diversas/livro_vermelho_2018_vol1.pdf>. Accessed on: 03 jun. 2019.

_____. Ministry of the Environment. *Brazilian Biodiversity*. Available at:
<http://www.mma.gov.br/biodiversidade/biodiversidade-brasileira>. Access on: 11 jun.
2019.

_____. *Glossary*. Available at: <http://www.mma.gov.br/component/k2/item/430-
gloss>. Accessed on: 10 jun. 2019.

_____. Chico Mendes Institute for Biodiversity Conservation - ICMBio. *Animal
trafficking contributes to the extinction of species*. Available at: <
http://www.icmbio.gov.br/portal/ultimas-noticias/4905-trafico-de-animais-contribui-
para-extincao-de-especies>. Access on: 18 nov. 2019.

BRAZIL. Ministry of Environment. *Precautionary Principle*. Available at:
<https://www.mma.gov.br/clima/protecao-da-camada-de-ozonio/item/7512>. Access
on: 26 Oct. 2019.

_____. *National System of Conservation Units* - SNUC. Available at:
<https://www.mma.gov.br/areas-protegidas/unidades-de-conservacao/sistema-
nacional-de-ucs-snuc.html>. Access on: 25 Oct. 2019.

BRAZILIAN INSTITUTE OF ENVIRONMENT AND RENEWABLE NATURAL
RESOURCES - IBAMA. *Brazilian Ecosystems*: study of ecological representativeness
in Brazilian biomes. Available at: <http://www.ibama.gov.br/>. Accessed on: 06 Jul.
2019.

ORGANIZATION OF THE UNITED NATIONS - UN. *The UN and the Environment*.
Available at: <https://nacoesunidas.org/acao/meio-ambiente/>. Accessed on: 26 Oct.
2019.

75

_____ . *Conferences on Environment and Sustainable Development*: a UN miniiguia. United Nations Brazil, 11 May 2017. Available at: <https://nacoesunidas.org/conferencias-de-meio-ambiente-e-desenvolvimento-sustentavel-miniguia-da-onu/>. Accessed on: 08 Jun. 2019.

_____ . Meet the UN. Available at: <https://nacoesunidas.org/conheca/>. Accessed on: 25 Oct. 2019.

_____ . *Convention on Biological Diversity*. United Nations, 1992, Art. 1. Available at <http://www.mma.gov.br/estruturas/sbf_dpg/_arquivos/cdbport.pdf>. Access on: 07 Mar. 2019.

_____ . *Declaration on Environment and Development*. 1992. Prepared by the United Nations Conference on Environment and Development. Available at: <http://www.dhnet.org.br/direitos/sip/onu/bmestar/rio92.htm>. Accessed on: 25 Oct. 2019.

_____ . The *UN report shows that 1 million species of animals and plants face extinction risk*. United Nations Brazil, 08 May 2019. Available at: <https://nacoesunidas.org/relatorio-da-onu-mostra-que-1-milhao-de-especies-de-animais-e-plantas-enfrentam-risco-de-extincao/>. Access on: 06 Jun. 2019.

RENCTAS. *1st National Report on Wildlife Trafficking*. Available at: <http://renctas.org.br/wpcontent/uploads/2014/02/REL_RENCTAS_pt_final.pdf>. Access on: 06 mar. 2019.

THE ECONOMICS OF ECOSYSTEMS AND BIODIVERSITY - TEEB. *Report for the Business Sector* - Executive Summary 01-07-2010. Available at: <http://www.mma.gov.br/publicacoes/biodiversidade/category/143-economia-dos-ecossistemas-e-da-biodiversidade.html?download=968:teeb-sumario-executivo>. Accessed on: 25 Oct. 2019.

UNITED NATIONS – UN. *EnvironmentProgramme*. Disponível em: <https://www.unenvironment.org/>. Acesso em: 25 out. 2019.

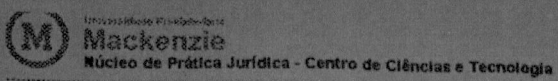

Mackenzie
Núcleo de Prática Jurídica - Centro de Ciências e Tecnologia

COORDENADORIA DE TCC

TERMO DE AUTENTICIDADE DO TRABALHO DE CONCLUSÃO DE CURSO

Eu, MATHEUS ZULIAN DOS SANTOS aluno(a), regularmente matriculado(a), no Curso de Direito, na disciplina do TCC da 10ª etapas matrícula nº 31518745 período MATUTINO, Turma F,tendo realizado o TCC com o título:TRÁFICO DE ANIMAIS SILVESTRES E CONSERVAÇÃO DA BIODIVERSIDADE: IMPACTOS, REGULAÇÃO E REPRESSÃO, sob a orientação do (a) professor (a): MÁRCIA BRANDÃO CARNEIRO LEÃO, declaro para os devidos fins que tenho pleno conhecimento das regras metodológicas para confecção do Trabalho de Conclusão de Curso (TCC), informando que o realizei sem plágio de obras literárias ou a utilização de qualquer meio irregular.

Declaro ainda que, estou ciente que caso sejam detectadas irregularidades referentes às citações das fontes e/ou desrespeito às normas técnicas próprias relativas aos direitos autorais de obras utilizadas na confecção do trabalho, serão aplicáveis as sanções legais de natureza civil, penal e administrativa, além da reprovação automática, impedindo a conclusão do curso.

Assinatura do(a) aluno(a)

Campinas,segunda-feira, 18 de Novembro de 2019